Prima Games

A Division of Random House, Inc.
3000 Lava Ridge Court
Roseville, CA 95661
1-800-733-3000
www.primagames.com

Associate Product Manager: Christy L. Curtis

Senior Project Editor: Brooke N. Hall

Editorial Assistant: Tamar D. Foster

Design: Gregory C. Han

ISBN: 0-7615-4083-0

Library of Congress Catalog Card Number: 2002112364

Printed in the United States of America

02 03 04 05 GG 10 9 8 7 6 5 4 3 2 1

PRIMA'S OFFICIAL

DAN EGGER

Welcome to Die Hard: Vendetta

You're about to find out what it's like to spend a day in the life of John McClane. Playing as the classic action hero from the *Die Hard* film trilogy, you are about to embark on another adventure and, like your previous endeavors, face insurmountable odds on your own.

The game takes you through a variety of locations, including an art museum, the LA sewers, a film studio, and a prison. By the time you're done, you'll feel like you've traveled halfway around the world and back.

At the heart of this story is your quest to rescue McClane's daughter, Lucy. She's no damsel in distress, though. She's a member of the Century City Police Department and as tough as her old man.

You'll need to be skilled to forge your way though *Die Hard: Vendetta*. Aside from besting the challenging design, you also have to master stealth tactics and solve problems with brains rather than bullets. But don't worry; you have plenty of weapons at your disposal, and we tell you how to use every one of them. Check out the gameplay tactics section before you start. The tips you'll find will give you an advantage over most players.

If you get stuck, this guide will get you out of trouble and help you with step-by-step instructions. Check out the guide even in areas you can easily conquer. The game is packed with cool secrets, and you don't want to miss one.

Codes

If you'd like a change of pace from the regular gameplay in *Die Hard: Vendetta*, try the following cheats. Enter each at the main menu, then start your game to play in whole new way.

Main menu

Liquid Metal

Ⓑ Ⓨ Ⓧ Ⓑ Ⓨ Ⓧ

This code turns all characters' skin into shiny liquid metal.

Hot Hands

Ⓑ Ⓨ Ⓛ Ⓛ

This code sets AI characters on fire when you punch them.

Kamikaze

Ⓛ Ⓡ Ⓩ Ⓨ Ⓑ

This code turns your bullets into incendiary rounds that explode on impact. It's great for taking out bad guys the easy way.

Exploding Fists

Ⓑ Ⓧ Ⓡ Ⓡ

This code makes AI characters explode when you punch them.

Flame On

Ⓑ Ⓧ Ⓧ Ⓑ Ⓧ Ⓧ

This code makes all the characters look like they're on fire. Don't worry, though, they won't burn you.

Invulnerable

Ⓛ Ⓡ Ⓛ Ⓡ Ⓛ Ⓡ Ⓛ Ⓡ

You'll be able to play through the game taking no damage when you use this code.

Big Heads

Ⓡ Ⓡ Ⓛ Ⓡ

This code inflates the heads of all the characters to make head shots easier. It also lowers the pitches of their voices.

Infinite Hero Time

Ⓑ Ⓧ Ⓧ Ⓩ Ⓛ Ⓡ

This code gives you unlimited Hero time. You can play through levels while the bad guys are moving in slow-mo.

Pin Heads

Ⓛ Ⓛ Ⓡ Ⓛ

If head shots are just too easy for you, try this code to shrink down your enemies' heads to a comically tiny size. They also talk in high-pitched voices.

All Levels

Ⓧ Ⓧ Ⓩ Ⓩ Ⓧ Ⓧ Ⓩ Ⓩ

This code unlocks every level in the game.

The Characters

John McClane

Former NYPD police officer John McClane transferred to Century City in order to be closer to his children after he and wife Holly divorced. Soon after the divorce, Holly was transferred to the Nakatomi offices in Japan, leaving John as sole parent.

Since the divorce, John has taken a quieter position in the department, spending most of his time behind a desk.

Lucy McClane

Daughter of John McClane and new graduate of the police academy, we have high hopes for Lucy's future with the department. She has proven to be a levelheaded individual who handles herself well in tense situations. Hopefully, she will become a star police officer in our ranks.

Captain Al Powell

Al Powell has risen to the rank of captain in the police department. Under his guidance, the CCPD has been able to clean up the department and move forward from our inconsistent and rocky past.

Dick Thornberg

This fast-talking, ambulance-chasing tabloid reporter has had numerous run-ins with the police department. He has been booked for obstruction of justice several times, and has made a career out of highlighting every problem and scandal within the department. Recently, he has taken a position as a reporter with the Hollywood Entertainment Network (H.E.N.). Hopefully, his new job will keep him away from the police.

Piet Gruber

Son of the notorious Hans Gruber, Piet is a spoiled, philandering playboy. While his quest for the good life keeps him very busy, we are keeping tabs on him.

Jack Frontier

Jack Frontier, the ex-Hollywood hard man, has been keeping a low profile since the critical panning of his last film. However, rumors abound that through his CIA and military background, he is taking a new direction as muscle for hire. Police department internal memo: Mark down for extra surveillance.

Marlin

A known ex-associate of Piet Gruber, Marlin has been in hiding since the failed hijacking of an oil tanker in the Persian Gulf, where she was positively identified as one of the main perpetrators. Intelligence sources believe she may have entered the country through Mexico, though her exact location is unknown. If spotted, approach with extreme caution.

Nitric

Explosives expert Nitric has spent more time inside prison than out of it. However, while inside, he accumulated an in-depth disregard for authority and the well-being of others. Nitric is a very dangerous individual. Fortunately, we currently have him in custody for a traffic misdemeanor.

Christophe Von Laben

Von Laben is the current curator at a prestigious Los Angeles art museum. He has been known to travel in the same circles as Gruber. While investigations have not found anything more to their relationship than art, we are still keeping them both under observation in connection with some high-level art thefts.

The Controls

Default Configuration

Knowing your controls is crucial to success in *Die Hard: Vendetta*. This section details every button you'll need in the game.

Action (Ⓐ)

This button is used for the following:
* Opening doors
* Talking to people
* Using floor-mounted miniguns
* Turning switches
* Activating control panels
* Taking a hostage

Switch Modes (Ⓑ)

This button switches you between Stealth Mode and Action Mode.

Crouch (Ⓧ)

This button puts you into a crouching position. If you hit it again, you return to a standing position. Double tap the crouch button to drop into a prone position.

Jump (Ⓨ)

This button enables you to jump. You can also use it to leap out of a crouch or prone position.

Hero Mode (🄻,Ⓨ)

The alternate function for the jump button switches you into Hero Mode, in which you move at regular speed, but your enemies move in slow motion.

Start (◯)

This button pauses the game and brings up your in-mission options menu.

Alternate Actions(🄻)

Holding this button switches some of your other buttons so that they have alternate functions. Check each button description for these secondary functions. This trigger also zooms in the view on weapons with a scope.

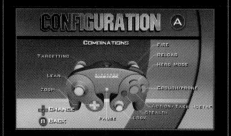

Fire (Ⓡ)

This button fires all of your weapons.

Reload (Ⓩ)

This button loads a new clip into your weapon. Use it after you use a bullet from your clip.

Movement and Strafe(◯)

The left joystick controls the direction in which you move. Moving this joystick left and right moves you in a sideways strafe.

Lean (🄻,◯)

When holding down these buttons, the left joystick allows you to lean around corners.

Check Inventory List (⬅)

This control brings up your inventory list.

Check Weapon List (➡)

This control brings up your weapons list.

Switch Weapons(⬆,⬇)

This searches through your weapons.

Zoom In and Out (L,©)	Look Up/Down and Turn (©)	Look Around (L,©)
Adjust your zoom using the D-Pad while holding L.	Control your head with ©.	Stay in one spot and look around. This button combo is good for aiming.

Other Configurations

If you're uncomfortable with the default settings, you can choose from two other button configurations.

Configuration B

Configuration C

The Weapons

The missions you face in *Die Hard: Vendetta* are challenging. Fortunately, you're equipped with some great weapons. This section provides more details about the weapons you encounter during your adventure.

Paintball Gun

While not deadly, the paintball gun is the standard police issue to get you through the yearly training evaluation.

Standard Ammo: Paintballs

Dual Mode: No

Advantages: The paintball gun won't hurt your fellow officers while you're in the training level.

Disadvantages: The paintball gun isn't used during the game's missions.

Tip: When your training evaluator is talking, paint the viewing window with the paintball gun for fun.

Revolver

Your standard police-issue weapon is a small, lightweight six-shot revolver.

Standard Ammo: 9mm full metal jacket

Dual Mode: Yes

Advantages: This is the gun that you start with, so it's the first one you'll grow accustomed to.

Disadvantages: The six-shot revolver means that you'll reload often. It's difficult to aim.

Tip: Reloading is your biggest concern with the revolver. Don't get caught out in the open with an empty clip.

9mm Pistol

Gruber's commandos use this 9mm semi-automatic pistol. It's reliable and packs a punch. It has a 17-round magazine and can be fitted with a silencer.

Standard Ammo: 9mm full metal jacket

Dual Mode: Yes

Advantages: The longer clip in the 9mm pistol means less reloading, and the semi-automatic firing mechanism is more accurate than fully automatic firing.

Disadvantages: The semi-automatic firing mechanism requires you to pull the trigger for each shot. It's slower than the automatic weapons.

Tip: Because you have to fire every shot, make each one count. Try for headshots whenever possible.

Silenced 9mm Pistol

This standard, 9mm semi-automatic pistol is a powerful stealth weapon when fitted with a silencer.

Standard Ammo: 9mm full metal jacket

Dual Mode: No

Advantages: The silenced 9mm pistol is quieter than any weapon, other than the crossbow. It's a great choice for those who like to play sneaky.

Disadvantages: This gun isn't totally silent. In missions that require you to remain undetected, this gun may give you away.

Tip: Stay in Stealth Mode as you move with this gun and only switch into Action Mode when you are stopped and ready to fire.

The Enforcer

Packing more power than the 9mm pistol, the Enforcer is a gas-powered handgun that does serious damage.

Standard Ammo: .50mm full metal jacket
Dual Mode: No
Advantages: This weapon has excellent stopping power.
Disadvantages: Ammo for the Enforcer is extremely rare.
Tip: Save the Enforcer for situations where you really need to take someone out with a single, quick shot.

9mm Submachine Gun

Lightweight and deadly, the 9mm submachine gun is best used with one in each hand. Be careful: It's powerful, but it goes through ammunition quickly.

Standard Ammo: 9mm full metal jacket
Dual Mode: Yes
Advantages: The 9mm submachine gun has an excellent rate of fire. It's especially handy in dual mode.
Disadvantages: This gun burns through ammo and is inaccurate at long distances.
Tip: Fire in short, controlled bursts so that your auto-target can reacquire your foe after you hit him with a couple bullets.

Tactical Submachine Gun

A vicious little 9mm, the tactical submachine gun is both simple and hardy, offering greater accuracy than the standard 9mm submachine gun.

Standard Ammo: 9mm full metal jacket
Dual Mode: Yes
Advantages: The tactical submachine gun is more accurate than the submachine gun and fires at a faster rate.
Disadvantages: This pistol isn't as accurate as the automatic rifles.
Tip: Keep a close eye on your crosshairs. When they turn red after locating a target, pull the trigger for a short burst of gunfire.

Assault Rifle

Renowned for its simple design and rugged construction, this rifle is reliable and easy to maintain. It uses a 30-round magazine.

Standard Ammo: 7.62 caliber full metal jacket
Dual Mode: No
Advantages: The assault rifle has better accuracy, a larger clip, and deadlier bullets than any of the pistols. It also has a minimal zoom feature for longer shots.
Disadvantages: It takes a long time to change a clip in the assault rifle.
Tip: Because of the long reload time, keep your clips full at all times by hitting reload at every break between enemy encounters.

High-Powered Assault Rifle

More powerful than a standard assault rifle, this rifle offers an adjustable scope for more precise shooting.

Standard Ammo: 7.62 caliber full metal jacket
Dual Mode: No
Advantages: The high-powered assault rifle has a fast rate of fire, great accuracy, and a useful scope.
Disadvantages: The high-powered assault rifle takes a long time to reload clips.
Tip: Use the scope to peek far ahead. In outdoor levels, you can spot enemies in the distance who can't see you. Take your time and kill them one at a time.

Sniper Rifle

It doesn't fire as rapidly as the high-powered assault rifle, but the sniper rifle is effective for long-distance shooting.

Standard Ammo: 7.62 caliber full metal jacket

Dual Mode: No

Advantages: The scope on the sniper rifle lets you take accurate long shots.

Disadvantages: The sniper rifle has a small clip and a long reload time.

Tip: A head shot does the same damage as three body shots, so it's worth the effort to line up a clean headshot.

Combat Shotgun

Need to cover a wide area with a single blast? Then the combat shotgun is for you. Powerful and deadly, it can blow through almost anything.

Standard Ammov Shotgun shells

Dual Mode: No

Advantages: The combat shotgun offers one-shot stopping power at short and medium ranges.

Disadvantages: The lag between shots from this weapon can get you in trouble during tense battles. The shotgun isn't useful over long distances.

Tip: When using the shotgun, follow a pattern of shooting, hiding, then shooting again. This gives your gun time to load another shell into the chamber.

Flamethrower

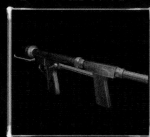

The flamethrower can take out several enemies at once. They also can't shoot at you while they're on fire.

Standard Ammo: Bottled Liquefied Gas

Dual Mode: No

Advantages: The flamethrower can take out large groups of enemies at once and incapacitate enemies on contact.

Disadvantages: You can suffer splash damage if the flame bounces off an object or wall. The flamethrower has a short firing range.

Tip: Save the flamethrower for situations where you're up against a group of enemies. Other weapons are more useful and safer in one-on-one conflicts.

Minigun

Miniguns are found in two forms: floor mounted and handheld. Miniguns let you lay down a lethal blanket of suppressive fire, decimating anything in your way.

Standard Ammo: 7.62 caliber full metal jacket

Dual Mode: No

Advantages: The minigun has a staggering rate of fire, and you never have to worry about running out of ammo.

Disadvantages: The floor-mounted minigun is difficult to aim, and you only get the handheld version at the end of the game.

Tip: When using a minigun, you can fire before you see an enemy. The gun is most effective when revved up to full speed.

Crossbow

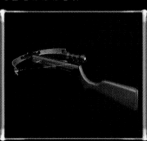

Silent and deadly, the crossbow is effective for taking out small groups of mercenaries. The latest models come fitted with sniper scopes.

Standard Ammo: Crossbow bolts

Dual Mode: No

Advantages: The crossbow is absolutely silent. It has a scope that's as useful as the sniper rifle's scope.

Disadvantages: The crossbow isn't very effective unless you score a head shot.

Tip: Use the crossbow to take out enemies hidden in the distance or in prime sniper locations. Don't use it for nearby enemies.

Rocket Launcher

Heavy and slow to load, the rocket launcher is capable of mass destruction.

Standard Ammo: Rockets

Dual Mode: No

Advantages: The rocket launcher is the most explosive weapon in the game, and the only one that can take out large targets, such as a helicopter or missile pad, with a single shot.

Disadvantages: If you fire a rocket in a tight area, there's a chance you'll kill yourself along with your enemies.

Tip: Only use the rocket launcher outdoors. It works well as an opening salvo when taking on a large group of enemies.

Fragmentation Grenade

The fragmentation grenade is filled with stainless steel wire that is blown in every direction when the grenade detonates.

Advantages: You can throw grenades around corners and over walls. They have a wide blast area that takes out multiple enemies.

Disadvantages: Grenades are difficult to aim and can cause you or a civilian hostage significant damage if you're not careful.

Tip: The longer you hold down the right trigger, the farther you'll throw the grenade. Experiment with this in the training level so you're comfortable with grenades during the game.

C4 and Trigger

The C4 and trigger allow you to set a charge where you want, and detonate it at will.

Advantages: C4 is useful because you can control exactly where you place the charge and exactly when it explodes.

Disadvantages: Because it requires a two-step process to fire (toss and trigger), C4 isn't as handy as a grenade.

Tip: Set up the C4 in a spot where you know your enemies will be, then trigger it when they hit the spot.

Proximity Mine

This explosive device has a built-in sensor that detonates the mine when anything gets too close. Be careful—that also includes you.

Advantages: You can leave proximity mines anywhere, and you don't have to detonate them yourself.

Disadvantages: Proximity mines can get you if you come too close to them.

Tip: Toss a proximity mine in the path of a patrolling enemy and let the explosives do the work for you.

VENDETTA

Items and Pick-Ups

Inventory Items

Inventory items are special power-ups you collect while on a mission. This section also details the mission items available in the game.

Medkit

Keep your eyes peeled for these kits, as they're essential to your survival. Pick them up and carry them with you until needed.

Use: Adds 50 points to your health, up to 100

Scarcity: Very common

Useful Tip: Only use a medkit when your health is near or below 50 points. Otherwise, you'll waste health points you may need later.

Rigel Optics 3200 Pro Night Vision Goggles

The Rigel 3200 Pro Night Vision Goggles give you a 100-yard visibility range in absolute darkness and 500 yards under a partial moon. They provide you with a 37-degree field of view, a built-in infrared illuminator, and Overlight protection circuitry.

Use: Enable you to see in the dark

Scarcity: Three in game

Useful Tip: Make sure that you're in a dark area before wearing the night vision goggles. If you wear them in a lighted area, the goggles will hamper your vision.

Body Armor

Armor does not completely protect you from certain types of damage, including damage you sustain from falling or running out of oxygen.

Use: Boosts your armor rating to 100, which protects your health rating until your armor declines to zero

Scarcity: Rare

Useful Tip: Doesn't make you invulnerable, but you can try more risky attacks if you're armored

SWAT Vest

The SWAT vest not only gives you the protection of the body armor, but also the added benefit that the police know on which side you are. This means your enemies will also know which side you're on.

Use: Boosts your armor points to 100 and acts as a SWAT team disguise

Scarcity: Very rare

Useful Tip: While wearing this item, play the same as you would while wearing regular body armor

Disguises

Disguises enable you to blend in and avoid confrontations.

Use: Enable you to fool people into thinking you're someone else

Scarcity: Three in game

Useful Tip: When wearing a disguise, do not call attention to yourself. If mercenaries see a hobo waving around dual 9mm pistols, they'll realize it's you.

Keys

Keys are helpful for opening locked doors and getting into areas that you couldn't earlier.

Use: Opens locked doors

Scarcity: Common

Useful Tip: You'll get keys most often by talking with characters in the game. Keep talking with the NPCs until they start repeating themselves. This way, you won't miss anything they might give away.

Blank Minigun Ammo Box

Throughout the game, miniguns need ammo only one time. When you see this box, grab it—it'll help you later.

Use: Loads ammunition for a certain minigun

Scarcity: One in the game

Useful Tip: Grab this when you find it and hold onto it

Circuit Breaker

A snip of a red or blue wire can't deactivate today's modern bombs. The high-tech circuit breaker disarms even the most advanced explosive devices.

Use: Allows you to punch in the codes to disarm bombs

Scarcity: One in the game

Useful Tip: Select your circuit breaker before you approach a bomb. Take your time and choose the right buttons to press. You'll have enough time to be careful.

Ammunition Pick-Ups

Throughout the game, you'll be able to pick up ammunition. For the most part, you'll pick up ammo by grabbing guns your enemies drop. However, you'll occasionally find other ammo. The following ammunition types are available in the game.

C4

This C4 belt contains both the C4 and the trigger.

Grenades

A belt of fragmentation grenades.

Proximity Mines

A belt of proximity mines.

13

Mission Items

Throughout the game you pick up important items that help you make your way through each mission. Every item has a purpose; so if you have it, you can use it.

* **Pool Club Card**–Use this to gain entrance to the Pool Club in the Hollywood Boulevard level. When the guy guarding the door asks you for your card, activate this in your inventory.

  Found in: **Level 2**

* **Painting Pieces**–Gather all three of these in the LA Sewers level.

  Found in: **Level 4**

* **Laptop**–After talking with Frontier, grab the laptop as evidence against him.

  Found in: **Level 4**

* **Evidence Briefcase**–At the end of the Century City Police Department level, you run across a mercenary holding a briefcase full of the evidence you collected in earlier levels. He drops it when you kill him.

  Found in: **Level 5**

* **Stage Swipe Card**–This card acts like keys to get you through a locked stage door. You don't need to activate it; cards automatically unlock doors.

  Found in: **Level 6**

* **Tin of Tuna**–You find a tin of Tuna in Nitric's prison cell. It doesn't do anything, but it is a hint about where you're headed next.

  Found in: **Level 7**

* **Cigarettes**–Offer these to the prisoner asking for a smoke in the Sierra Correctional Facilities and he gives you a Lit Cigarette.

  Found in: **Level 7**

* **Lit Cigarette**–Use this to light a mattress in one of the other prison cells. The fire distracts the guards and helps you escape.

  Found in: **Level 7**

* **Safe Combination**–Without this combination, you can't open the safe hidden behind a painting in the warden's office. Good thing he left it lying on the floor.

  Found in: **Level 7**

* **Asbestos Gloves**–In the freezer section of the Cesar Tuna Factory, you need to wear these gloves to protect your hands after you use your flamethrower to unthaw a frozen door handle.

  Found in: **Level 8**

* **Clipboards**–These have important information written on them. Activate them on your inventory screen to see what they say.

  Found in: **Level 9**

* **Keypad Code**–This code opens a door in the Fernandez Warehouse.

  Found in: **Level 9**

* **Detonator Code**–A guard carries this on the top floor of the Nakatomi Building. Activate it in your inventory screen when standing near Lucy to save her from an untimely death.

  Found in: **Level 10**

* **Walkie Talkies**–Use these to talk with anyone on the same frequency. Sometimes it's the police, and other times it's the bad guys. Activate the walkie talkie in your inventory to talk on them.

  Found in: **Levels 10 and 11**

* **Explosive Ammo**–Find this on the upper ring of the observatory while you fight Frontier. Use this to reload your assault rifle.

  Found in: **Level 11**

Gameplay

In *Die Hard: Vendetta*, you can choose from three gameplay modes: Action Mode, Stealth Mode, and Hero Mode. Each mode plays an important role in how you progress through the game. Knowing when and where to use each one is often the difference between success and failure.

Action Mode

In *Die Hard: Vendetta*, you're in Action Mode more often than in any other mode. Get comfortable with it; you'll need to be an action hero to make it to the end.

Action Mode Advantages

In Action Mode, you can run faster, jump farther, and move more quickly than in Stealth Mode. More importantly, you can shoot only in Action Mode. If you can't see your crosshairs, you're probably in Stealth Mode.

Action Mode Disadvantages

In Action Mode, you make a lot of noise when you move. Even moving slowly, you'll be identified by the enemy. Also, the speed of Action Mode makes any kind of careful movement on elevated paths very risky.

The Crosshairs

Before you start Die Hard: Vendetta, you can choose your own set of crosshairs. Choose the one that fits your style of gameplay. Here are a few recommendations:

The Sniper

Don't choose a set of crosshairs that impairs your view or fails to precisely define the center of your target. Instead, choose a set that is smaller and includes a center marker for your most precise shots.

The Gunner

If you prefer to use auto-target, pick a larger set of crosshairs so you can spot when they turn red for a positive target lock-on.

The Balanced Player

You can find several balanced crosshairs; so find a set that works best for you and doesn't get in your way while playing.

Action Mode Tips

* When moving through levels with tight corridors, stay in Action Mode to shoot anyone who pops out at you.

* Make sure your longer jumps are in Action Mode.

* Activate a weapon so that you can see a set of crosshairs. Use them to carefully aim your leap.

* Use your crosshairs to check out trouble in the distance and around corners. Many times your auto-target spots enemies before you can.

Stealth Mode

Throughout *Die Hard: Vendetta*, you'll find many opportunities to use Stealth Mode to your advantage. If you're comfortable using Stealth Mode rather than shooting your way through trouble, you'll find that many of the solutions to your problems are easy and clever. For instance, many hostage situations can be solved by sneaking up, grabbing the enemy leader, and arresting the bad guys without firing a bullet.

Stealth Mode Advantages

In Stealth Mode, the enemy can't hear or see you, even if you walk behind him or her. This mode allows you to grab enemies from behind and arrest or kill them. This is an important tactic throughout the game.

Stealth Mode is useful for jumping and traversing narrow pathways. If you want to move safely, Stealth Mode makes it easier.

Stealth Mode Disadvantages

In Stealth Mode, you're slower than in Action Mode and you can't jump as far. Also, your weapons aren't immediately ready to fire. If you're attacked, you'll lose time preparing to fire your weapon.

The Grab

One of the coolest things about Die Hard: Vendetta is the grabbing feature. If you're holding a one-handed weapon or no weapon at all, you can grab enemy players by sneaking up behind them when they look in another direction.

To grab someone from behind, switch into Stealth Mode using Ⓑ and approach your target. When you're close enough to grab him, the figure in your damage meter flashes red.

When the icon flashes red, hit Ⓐ to reach out and grab the person you're standing behind. You can only grab someone when the icon is flashing red.

The Takedown

After you grab an enemy, you have a couple of options. Choose the one that's best for your situation.

Arrest the Bad Guy

After you grab an enemy, arrest him by hitting Ⓐ. This forces him to the ground and cuffs him in place. Other police officers will pick him up later. When arrested, the character is left kneeling. Depending on his position, you may be able to hit Ⓐ and interrogate him.

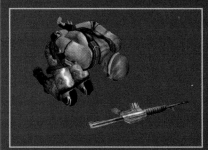

Head down: Can't be interrogated.

Head up: Can be interrogated.

Use the Leader to Arrest Others

If you grab an enemy, you can drag him over to other bad guys. If you grab the leader, they throw down their weapons and surrender without a fight. If you grab a regular bad guy, they shoot.

The key to hostage taking is knowing how to spot an enemy leader. Here are three hints for spotting a leader:

* The leader dresses differently from the other troops.

* The leader is the first enemy you encounter when sneaking up on a group.

* Except for the first one, the leader wears a ball cap.

The other bad guys are arrested after you grab their weapons and they're kneeling on the ground.

Kill the Bad Guy

To kill the enemy you've grabbed, press ⬜ when he or she is in your grasp. If you're holding a gun to his head, you'll shoot him in the head. If you're using your fists, you'll snap his neck.

Stealth Mode Tips

* If you hear the bad guys talking, switch into Stealth Mode. Sneak up on your enemies while they're distracted by a conversation.

* Carry a one-handed weapon when you grab an enemy. Nothing's worse than sneaking up behind someone and not being able to grab him because both your hands are full.

* Switch to Stealth Mode when you walk over areas where there's a danger of falling, or to jump on something. It's much safer and easier than Action Mode.

Hero Mode

Perhaps the coolest mode of all in *Die Hard: Vendetta* is Hero Mode. This feature enables you to slow time while you move at full speed. Use this mode to take down large groups of enemies or bosses.

Hero Mode Advantages

When time slows in Hero Mode, your enemies can't easily shoot you. Also, you can pick your targets and the exact position where you'll aim.

You're not invincible in Hero Mode, but if you use it correctly, you can eliminate anyone without taking much damage yourself.

Hero Mode Disadvantages

You can only use Hero Mode when you've acquired hero points (see sidebar, "Gathering Hero Points"). If you only have a few hero points, you won't have much Hero Mode time to play with. Also, Hero Mode runs until it uses up your hero points.

Gathering Hero Points

Each time you save a hostage, you accumulate hero points. The bar on the left side of your health meter fills up with red as your hero points rise.

Switching into Hero Mode

To switch into Hero Mode, hold down ⬜ and hit ✕. You'll hear music and a whooshing sound effect, then the game slows. Act before your hero time runs out.

Hero Mode Tips

* Save every hostage you see, even if it doesn't help you finish the level. Hero points are too valuable to pass up.

* When fighting large groups in Hero Mode, fire a couple of bullets into each enemy, then move on. If you wait for them to die and fall in slow motion, you'll waste your time.

* When fighting a boss in Hero Mode, aim for the head and fire.

Tactics

You'll face many challenging missions throughout *Die Hard: Vendetta* , and you'll need to develop tactics that will help you make it through the game. Here are 10 tactics that will serve you well.

Keep an Eye on Your Clip

One of the most common ways that players lose health points is by stepping into a battle without a full clip. If you're reloading while the bad guys are shooting at you, you're going to take damage.

Keep your clip reloaded whenever you aren't fighting. And when you're in the middle of a battle, it's better to hide and reload than to run out of bullets and let the auto-reload feature do it for you while you're standing in harm's way.

Fire in Short Bursts

Even though there are many fully automatic weapons in this game, don't use them like they do in the movies. If you hold down the trigger and spray your enemies, you'll waste bullets. You'll also find that your auto-target doesn't lock on while you're holding down the trigger.

Instead, fire in second-long bursts (enough to release a lethal grouping of bullets). Doing this allows the auto-target to acquire new enemies each time you fire, and you save ammo. You can also chew through large groups of enemies.

Stick and Move

Although it seems like a no-brainer to avoid standing in the open during the middle of a firefight, many players do exactly that when a large group of enemies confronts them. Take your enemies out one at a time, hiding and reloading after each kill.

You can clear many rooms before you even enter. Stand by either side of the entrance, peek in, cut loose on a single target with a short burst of fire, then hide. Do this correctly and you can make it through numerous battles without taking damage.

Help Your Auto-Target

At the game's easiest difficulty level, the auto-target picks up enemies anywhere on the screen. In tougher difficulty levels, however, that lock-on window shrinks. Because hitting an enemy using auto-target is easier than aiming, assist your auto-target.

To do this, make sure your crosshairs are close to an enemy's location when you spot him or her. If you know that a bad guy is waiting for you on a level above or below you, aim your crosshairs to that general elevation before stepping into the open where you can get a clean shot. If you don't, your auto-target struggles to locate the enemies while you get hit by their gunfire.

Aim for the Head

Each head shot does more damage than a regular body shot. The only problem is that the auto-target focuses on your enemy's chest. To take out a bad guy, use L and manually aim at his head. Use this technique for your opening salvo on a group of bad guys to save ammo for your next kill.

Aiming for the head is important when using the sniper rifle and crossbow. A head shot is as damaging as three body shots, so take your time and get a good clean shot. It's worth the extra seconds it may take to line up your sights.

Look for Alternate Approaches

One of the coolest things about the game is the fact that many of the tougher situations have alternate solutions that reward clever thinking. When you're faced with a dangerous situation or you see something that looks out of the ordinary, step back and look for another way to solve the problem. In this game, the alternate solution is often easier than the straightforward approach.

One trick is to look for interactive objects that can help you out. Whether it is a canister of liquid nitrogen, a flowerpot you can drop onto an enemy, or elevator doors that don't close right, when you see something that stands out, experiment with it to see if it might help you.

Use Stealth Whenever Possible

For most of the game, using stealth is easier than fighting your way through tough situations. When you come across bad guys in the middle of a conversation, switch to Stealth Mode. You should be able to identify the leader and grab him.

Grabbing and arresting bad guys either one at a time or in a group is safer than trying to win a shootout. Even in the best shootouts, you might take a bullet, but you'll rarely get damaged while arresting bad guys.

Use the Stealth Trick

When fighting enemies at medium to long distances, you can hide from your foes in Stealth Mode even if they were just shooting at you. The trick is to move only in Stealth Mode.

For instance, if you're fighting a group of bad guys in the distance, duck out of view and switch to Stealth Mode. Move to another location, stand, switch to Action Mode without moving your left joystick. Aim, open fire on your target, and hide. In some cases, you can repeat this process again and again until your enemies are dead.

Use Hero Points

At the beginning of each level, your hero points revert to zero, so use them up at the end of each mission. In later missions, save your hero points for a tough section or boss battle, but in early levels, you might accidentally save them for a crisis that never comes.

Whenever you face a boss, you know that it's time to use your hero points because the level ends when you beat the boss. Don't use your hero points before you're ready to shoot at the boss. Don't waste valuable hero time scrambling into position.

Efficiently Use Medkits

Medkits are common in this game, but that doesn't mean that you should be careless with them. A medkit gives you 50 health points, up to 100. If you use a medkit when your health is at 70, you'll only boost your health to 100, for a total of 30 health points. When you do this, you're throwing away 20 health points.

Instead, use a medkit when your health is at or below 50. This way, you squeeze every health point out of each medkit. In boss situations and a few dangerous encounters, however, ignore this rule and start the encounter with 100 health.

VENDETTA

Level 1:
TOWNSEND MUSEUM

John McClane's daughter is caught in a bloody multimillion-dollar art heist, and he's the only man who can save the day.

Daddy's girl is in big trouble.

OBJECTIVES

* **Avoid non-hostile casualties.**

* **Rescue Lucy McClane.**

* **Save any other hostages.**

Don't shoot a civilian or your game's over.

Start at the entrance to Townsend Museum, and you'll see several frightened civilians and police officers. Take time to talk to each one. They know you by name and reputation, and some have information about your mission.

Talk now—there won't be time for gabbing when the action starts.

Look next to Claudia Sherman, the frazzled valley girl in the blue halter-top, to find a medkit. Pick it up.

Take her medkit.

Find Sergeant Al Powell, and talk with him. As your conversation progresses, he fills you in on what's going on and alerts you that the door is open. Until you talk with him, it stays closed.

This is Sergeant Powell.

TIP!

Aim for your enemy's head. It's easier to take him down this way, often with a single shot.

Go through the gate and enter the museum. Step through the opening and get out of the way. The door caves in, and if you dally you take damage.

Don't get hit by the falling debris.

Walk to the doors on your left. Sometimes a mercenary pops out from behind the doors and shoots. If he doesn't, sneak to the doors and shoot him through the glass.

Be careful, he can see through the glass, too.

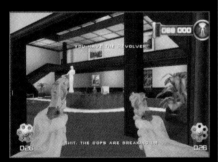

Use the dead mercenary's gun to kill more mercenaries.

Before you enter the main lobby area, pick up your second revolver so that you're loaded for double-barrel action. Two mercenaries are on the floor level and another is on the level above. Take them out from the bottom level.

Get the enemies on the ground floor first, then take out the enemy upstairs.

Inside the lobby desk is a medkit. Grab it even if you have full health; it's useful later.

The receptionist keeps the medkits close.

Proceed up the staircase that splits in two directions, and take the stairs on the right. Take out the mercenary in the top room.

Take out the mercenary and hide in the room where he was.

You encounter two more mercenaries on the upper level. Take them out one at a time. Get the one in the closest corner first, then shoot the other before he attacks you from a different angle. When you're done, head through the glass door.

The exit is at the end of the balcony on your left.

TIP!

To conserve ammo, fire in short, quick bursts.

Head down the hallway to the gallery. Before you step into the second room, a mercenary walks by.

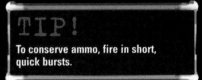

Get the first mercenary as soon as possible.

Shoot the first mercenary from a distance. Wait until the second one comes into the doorway, then shoot him. If you rush into the room, you may hit the hostage with stray bullets.

Attack the second mercenary from a distance to avoid hurting the hostage.

Two 9mms are better than one.

Pick up both mercenaries' guns so you can use dual 9mm pistols. They have much bigger clips than the revolvers, which means less reloading in the middle of a battle.

Hostages equal hero points.

Talk to the hostage to score a hero point. As you collect these points, you can go into Hero Mode for longer periods of time. Don't use Hero Mode to slow the game down now, save it until you're in a situation where you're hopelessly outgunned.

TIP!

Hero Mode slows your enemy's speed and gives you sharper reflexes. Hero Mode can't be shut off until it has run its course.

Three million dollars a shot.

Take a few pop shots at the priceless Ming vases in the museum displays. You can't do this in real life, so appreciate it while you can.

Liberate the hostage, then leave the room and walk into a narrow hall. Mercenaries ambush you from the left. Stay in the hall and dispatch the two shooters from a distance. If necessary, duck for cover along the wall.

Stay in the corridor until they're dead.

Next, step onto the balcony and turn right. There's an enemy directly in front of you, and one across the balcony. Take them out.

One's on your right and the other's ahead and to your left.

Item!

This level's third medkit lies at the top of the stairs. With all three, you can make it through the toughest scrapes.

Don't forget your medkit.

Take the stairs down to a small courtyard. An enemy is across the courtyard from the staircase. Circle around the outside edge to catch the mercenary who's trying to find you. Act quickly to take him out while he's facing away from you.

Stay outside and circle. He won't know what hit him.

The other courtyard mercenary is hiding under the stairs. Ambush him to prevent a surprise attack.

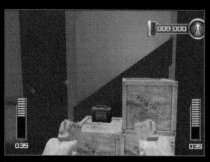

Kill the mercenary under the stairs.

Item!

A Sniper Rifle is sitting on top of the crates. Grab it. Your hostages will thank you later.

The coolest weapon in the level.

After you defeat the two mercenaries, a reporter bursts out of the double doors and starts talking. Converse with him, but keep your eyes on the doors behind him—more bad guys are on their way.

Talk all you want, but watch the door.

Stay where you are in the courtyard and gun down the two mercenaries that pop around the corner.

TIP!

When grabbing a bad guy, grab the one that looks like a leader. He's usually by himself and dressed differently from the others.

Two quick bursts of gunfire, and they both go down.

Turn the corner and you come across a lone mercenary. John McClane makes a comment about him being the mercenary leader. You can take him out or follow one of two alternate stealth paths. We'll follow the straightforward approach, but if you want to be sneaky, see sidebars, "Alternate Path 1" and "Alternate Path 2."

Deal with this mercenary and his buddies...the easy way or the hard way.

Alternate Path 1

Grabbing the mercenary makes your life easier later on. Sneak behind him in Stealth Mode. When the icon on the right of your health meter is flashing red, hit the action button to grab him.

Make sure you see the flashing icon before you grab.

Next, drag the mercenary leader into the room where Von Laben, the art dealer, is being held. The mercenary leader tells the other mercenaries to disarm. Drag the mercenary leader to each of his underlings, one by one. They drop to their knees, and you have them arrested. At that point, Von Laben is free.

Get their leader, and they surrender.

Alternate Path 2

If you grab the mercenary leader, you can try another trick to free Von Laben. Instead of taking the leader into the room, drag him into the courtyard where you talked to the reporter, then shoot him in the head. It's not sporting, but it's effective.

One shot, short and sweet.

When you reach the room where Von Laben is being guarded, he won't be held at gunpoint. He's lightly guarded by four mercenaries, so you won't have to use sharp-shooting tactics. Spray the guards with your double 9mm pistols.

Without a boss, these guys are clueless when it comes to hostage guarding.

If you decide to attack the bad guys head on, you're doing things the hard way. After you take out the leader, slide to the room's left side and peek into the doorway. Shoot a couple of guys, and others run toward you.

Move slowly and hit them before they spot you.

Take out the guard holding Von Laben. If your shot's not accurate, you'll kill the hostage instead. Use your Sniper Rifle for the cleanest shot.

Now it's just you and this poor fellow.

Don't shoot the mercenary from a long distance with regular weapons, but don't get too close to the hostage. If you do, the mercenary kills him.

Get a clean shot and take it.

Clear the area, then talk to Von Laben. He wants his art back.

All Von Laben wants to do is talk and hide.

Double the damage, double the ammo usage.

Pick up the mercenaries' Submachine Guns to arm yourself with the best weapons in this level. Watch the ammo, though; it runs out quickly in the heat of combat.

After you talk with Von Laben, exit to a balcony on your left. Switch to the dual submachine guns. Make sure they're fully loaded; you need every bullet for this last part.

This guy's about to find out that smoking kills.

Take out the mercenary on the balcony, and run down the stairs to your left. Make your stand from the corner of the court-yard at the bottom of the stairs.

Make your stand in a place where your back is protected.

Several enemies come at you, so prepare to take out anything that moves. When it's clear, head to the other side of the court-yard and look for enemies standing on the platform. As you move along the railing, you'll see a couple.

You can hit them, but they usually can't hit you.

Watch the location where the courtyard opens into the next part of the outdoor area. Several mercenaries come at you, but if you target one spot, you'll wipe them out when they get there.

Target first...

...then take them out.

When the area is clear, exit the courtyard and head toward the helicopter. Let it go.

No sense in taking pot shots at the fleeing helicopter.

Another medkit lies behind two crates in the area between the outdoor areas. Check your health—you may need it immediately.

One last medkit for the road.

There are mercenaries around the helicopter. Take them out from the connecting segment between the two areas. When it seems like you've got them all, there's still one guy left.

You've almost got it cleared!

The last mercenary is guarding Lucy. Use any weapon with the left trigger or Sniper Rifle to take that final shot. If you hit him, he releases Lucy and you can take him out. Or, try another way....

Alternate Path 3

To avoid the dangerous shot, shoot the hanging plant over his head. When it falls, it distracts him and he lets go of Lucy. Shoot him with a submachine gun.

Just shoot the plant...

...to divert the mercenary.

Talk with Lucy and the reporter. When you're done, you're ready for the next level.

This guy is nothing but trouble.

Level 2:
Hollywood Boulevard

Hollywood Boulevard: Part One

OBJECTIVES

* **Avoid civilian casualties.**

* **Respond to police calls.**

You begin on a sidewalk next to a police barrier. Take a moment and talk to the guy behind the barrier to get a feel for what you're about to face.

You can always trust the milkman.

As you walk toward the main street, talk with the girl on the sidewalk. If you have your gun out, she'll get angry. If you're in Stealth Mode, you might even get to flirt a little.

The bad way to pick up chicks.

The better way to pick up chicks.

Now head to the end of the sidewalk and take a left. (It's the only direction you can go.) Fat Larry the diner owner pulls out a gun and shouts. Talk with him to calm him down.

Fat Larry needs to relax a little.

After you talk with Fat Larry, walk into the diner and talk with a few patrons. When you reach the table with the two dead gang members, John McClane speaks for a moment. Be ready, this means some gang members are returning to the diner.

Be prepared, trouble's coming.

TIP!

Don't grab the medkit until after you dispatch the three gang members. If you grab it too early, they may end up having a shootout with Fat Larry. If they kill him, you have to start over.

When McClane makes his statement about the gang member's colors and army boots, turn around and aim your gun at the door. A civilian enters, followed by three gang members. Take them out.

Diner takedown: Straightforward approach.

Alternate Stealth Approach

If you don't want to engage in needless gunfire, try hiding behind the cash register until the three gang members enter the diner. When they walk by, sneak behind them and grab the leader.

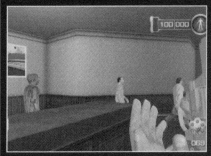

The leader is the guy in the hat.

Wait until the body icon in the upper right corner of the screen flashes red, then grab the leader. Walk him to the other gang members and they drop their weapons and surrender.

See? No wasted bullets!

Afterward, hit the action button and the leader will be arrested, too. You can interrogate them if you like, but you won't squeeze much info out of these bad guys.

The other cops will pick them up later.

Item!

This level's first medkit sits in the back of the diner. Wait until after you take out the three gang members before you grab it.

Fat Larry keeps a medkit near the kitchen.

After you dispatch the three gang members, go outside and turn right when you hit the sidewalk. If you want to have fun, turn right into the first alley you encounter and break up a lovers' tryst.

Don't hassle them. Even if you punch the guy, the level's over.

When you're through with the lovers, return to the sidewalk and take a right. Eventually you reach a standoff between the police and some gang members in front of a bank.

When you see the police cars, be ready to fight.

TIP!

If you don't want to bother with Hero Points, skip the diner confrontation altogether and head straight to the bank.

Shoot at the gang members in front of the bank as quickly as you can. If you wait too long, a cop dies and you have to restart the level. When you get there, you see three perpetrators shooting at police and another holding a hostage at gunpoint.

Target the gunmen first.

First, take out the three perpetrators with guns, then focus your attention on the guy holding the hostage. You can approach him for a clean shot, but don't get any closer than a few feet behind the two pillars nearest him.

Come any closer and the hostage is dead.

Use the targeting trigger to get the best aim possible so you can get a clean shot. He doesn't give you many opportunities and you'll need good aim, but you can take him out with a little patience.

Carefully aim and make sure to stay clear of the hostage.

Alternate Approach

If you don't want to risk hitting the hostage, there's a better way to take out the perpetrator. Instead of shooting the bad guy, aim at the screen of the ATM machine closest to him.

Aim at the flashing green screen.

When you hit the ATM screen, it explodes and the machine shoots out money. This distracts the perpetrator and he lets go of the hostage, making himself an easy target for you and your friends.

Money!

Now that he's clear, finish him off. Even if you miss, the other cops should do the job for you.

This level's easiest takedown.

Inside the bank, you'll find a group of hostages. Talk with them for a while. They're unhappy with their current situation. When you're done, slowly work your way up the stairs.

Call an ambulance for this guy by looking at him and hitting the action button.

After you reach the first landing on the stairs, turn and run to the top of the stairs, then through the door to the right. While you're running, a hostage sprints out of the door, followed by a bad guy.

If you wait even a moment, the hostage will be shot.

To survive, you need to take out the first bad guy as quickly as possible. Then, take the aforementioned door on the right and go through another door on your immediate right. There's a bad guy in this safe room, so take care of him.

Take out the two bad guys.

Alternate Stealth Approach

If you walk up the stairs in Stealth Mode, you can eavesdrop on a conversation between a hostage and one of his assailants. If you listen long enough, the hostage punches the perpetrator and runs to freedom.

Nice swing.

Go to the top of the stairs, take the door on your right, then make an immediate right. Another bad guy is in the safe room; you can take him out quickly.

Remember to thank the hostage later.

Once you're in the safe room, turn around and defend the door. Several bad guys approach the door. Shoot them all.

The bodies tend to pile up quickly.

TIP!

Fight from the safe room, where you'll only have one entrance to defend. There are so many bad guys upstairs that you'll find it hard to take them out in the open without getting shot in the back.

Directly across from the safe room is another room with an overturned desk in it. There's a perpetrator crouching behind the desk. Shoot him through the glass before you enter the room.

Shoot him from outside the room.

Jump onto the file cabinet on the far side of the room, then jump out the broken window to finish Part One of this level.

Two jumps and you're out.

 Level 2:
Hollywood Boulevard

Hollywood Boulevard: Part Two

OBJECTIVES

* Avoid civilian casualties.

* Interrogate gang members to find out their leader's name.

* Apprehend Fat Larry's assailant.

* Infiltrate the gang meeting.

You begin in an alley, where you'll hear a man pleading for his life. Take a right (a▮▮▮▮ the locked gate) into the main alleyway. If you look just past the broken, bloody ladder, you'll see a short alley on your left.

There's trouble around the corner.

You'll see a man being held up by three gunmen. If you want to take them by force, head back in the alley and target the g▮▮ the center. If you don't shoot him first, he'll kill the hostage. Shoot the other two immediately after.

When your crosshairs turn from red to white, quit shooting so you don't hit the hostage.

> # TIP!
>
> You'll eventually need to interrogate a gang member, and this is your easiest opportunity. Try Alternative Stealth Approach 2 for the simplest way to catch and interrogate these criminals.

Alternate Stealth Approach 1

Switch into Stealth Mode, run right to the thug in the middle, and grab him when your icon flashes red. Make the other two bad guys drop their weapons, and arrest and interrogate them.

It's risky, but you can make a quick run and grab.

> # TIP!
>
> When trying to grab a gunman, make sure that you're in Stealth Mode and that you're only holding one gun. If you have two showing, you don't have a free hand to grab with.

Alternate Stealth Approach 2

An easier way to apprehend all three suspects is to enter the alley in Stealth Mode and hide out of view behind the wall on the left of the alley.

Wait right here.

When you're safely in place, fire back into the area you just came from. The leader of the thugs sends the other two to investigate the noise. They run right past you.

They never check behind themselves.

With them out of the way, you can easily approach and capture the leader. Drag him out to the street, and the other two will surrender as well. Apprehend and interrogate them.

Don't forget to question the gunmen.

After you take care of the criminals and talk with the hostage, head to the main alley and take a left. At the end of this alley is a trash bin. Jump on top of it.

You'll need this trash bin to get on the roof.

From atop the trash bin, jump onto the closest roof, then make the hop onto the roof next to it. Next, jump to the ledge on the other side of the alley by running toward it and letting the auto-jump kick in when you reach the edge.

With auto-jump, it's easy to get on this ledge.

TIP!

You aren't required to use auto-jump for longer leaps, but it's safer than trying to do it the other way. Rely on the auto-jump feature.

Walk along the ledge until you reach a platform area. From this point, jump across the smaller alley to the roof doorway on the other side.

It looks dangerous, but you can make the jump easily.

Enter the doorway and walk down the stairs. The stairs make a U-turn, and at the very bottom is a small room with a gunman inside. He will pop into the doorway as soon as you start toward the room. Shoot him quickly.

Have your cursor aimed at head level before he even shows up.

Exit through the other door in the room, and a gunman pops out at you from the end of a short hallway. If you're prepared, he'll be an easy target.

Keep your finger on the trigger from the moment you start down the stairs.

Exit the building. When you hit the main sidewalk, take a right. (A left takes you to the pool hall, but first, you need a key card and disguise to get in.)

Head this way and take care of business.

When you walk near the Fashion Outlet, you'll hear some gang members talking. They have two hostages you'll want to save.

You're outnumbered. Be careful.

Switch to Stealth Mode and sneak in through the door or the broken window in the front of the store. Sneak up to a position where there's a clothes rack between you and the guy with the baseball cap. Shoot the other two guys, then kill him.

Save him for last–he's the least likely to shoot the hostages.

TIP!

Unless you really want to take the level with guns blazing, try the alternate stealth approach. You can kill all three gunmen without hurting the hostages, but it's very risky.

Alternate Stealth Approach

The best way to take down these subjects is to sneak into the store in Stealth Mode and grab the leader in the hat.

He's the leader, grab him first

After you arrest these guys, they're more than happy to give you all the information you need. If you killed the first group of gunmen in this level, it's very important that you interrogate these guys.

They'll gladly give you the name of their boss.

Item!

Talk to the hostages, then walk to the counter behind them to find a gang disguise. You can put it on now or save it for later.

Time for a costume change.

Walk back into the dressing area, where there's a row of changing rooms. The first and last are empty. The third one from the entrance has a thug hiding in it. Open the curtain and eliminate him.

Third cubicle from the entrance.

Open the second changing room to find a surprise.

Well, hello!

Leave through the back door of the changing area to enter a back alley. Four gunmen are loading a truck, and they'll attack you on sight. Take them all out.

Make sure you get all four gunmen.

Item!

There's a medkit inside the semi at the far end. Grab it for later on.

Sweet, sweet medkit.

Now open the door on the brown brick building. You will be in the back store-room of the Music Store. Open the next door, and you'll see the store clerk (don't shoot him) and a gunman crouched below (shoot him).

Be careful with your shot, the hostage might get in the way.

Item!

The thug drops a Pool Club Card. Pick it up–you'll need it very soon.

Membership has its privileges.

After you get the Pool Club Card, dress in the gang costume (you'll see the sleeves on your arms). Jump over the counter, and head to the main sidewalk.

All dressed up with somewhere to go.

Alternate Approach

You can go through the Music Store before you enter the Fashion Outlet if you like. It's worth it to watch the store clerk hint to you that there's a gang member under his counter.

Pay attention to his hints.

Now that you're outside, follow the sidewalk back the way you came (left if you're facing the street). You arrive at the Pool Club.

It's time for some infiltration.

Head up the stairs and talk with the receptionist. If you're dressed in the gang disguise and activate the Pool Club Card, he'll buzz you in and you can go inside.

The gang headquarters.

There are quite a few gang members in the room and some rival troops on their way. So, have both guns fully loaded and be ready for some intense action.

The gunfight.

Item!

One of the gang members will drop Keys to the Chinese Cinema. You'll need these to exit the level.

It's like having free movie passes.

Alternate Stealth Approach

If you don't want to fight your way through the gang

Order a drink while you wait.

A rival gang breaks into the Pool Club, and a gunfight ensues. Stay out of harm's way and clean up the survivors.

Let the gangs do the hard work for you.

Item!

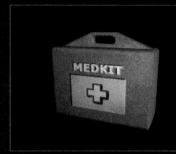

Behind the bar is a medkit. It will help fix the wounds you might have received so far.

The bartender likes to keep a medkit handy.

When all the gang members are dead, head out of the Pool Club. Eliminate the three gunmen in the parking lot.

Keep shooting and keep moving.

Next, head down the sidewalk toward the Music Store. A gunman will jump out from in front of Hooper's Pawnbrokers. Another will jump out from in front of the Lime Lite. Kill them both.

Don't let him scare you.

You'll end up at a large ditch in the middle of the sidewalk. Two thugs are waiting in the ditch. Take them out.

Alternate Approach

If you want to have a little fun, jump into the tractor that sits to the right of the pit and hit the action button.

Jump in the tractor and activate it

The tractor dumps its load of debris on the gang members, and you won't have to shoot them.

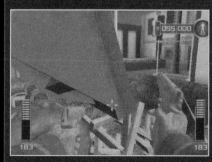

A job well done.

When the gang members are dead, go past the ditch and wipe out the five gang members standing in front of the Chinese Cinema.

Don't let any of them get behind you.

Use the Keys to open the theater door and exit the level.

Level 3:
The Chinese Cinema

Chinese Cinema: Part One

OBJECTIVES

* Avoid civilian casualties.
* Track down the lost art.
* Free captured employees.

You start at the entrance to the Chinese Cinema. Whatever you do, don't open the door leading into the theater lobby. If you open it, the hostage will be crushed under a pile of debris.

What a terrible way to die.

Instead, shoot out one of the red windows and the crooks will come running. Stay in the foyer and don't kill any enemies until they enter the small room you're in. Otherwise, you'll run out of bullets too quickly.

Let the bad guys come to you.

After you kill the eight bad guys, jump through one of the glass windows and free the theater employee. (Be careful—you might think you're done after killing six, but there are two more upstairs that sometimes lag behind the others, and another two that stay in the bathroom.)

Quick, convenient carnage.

TIP!

Remember, if you open the door from inside the foyer at any time, the debris will fall from the ceiling. So, be careful and free the hostage as quickly as possible.

If you want to make sure that you've gotten everyone, two more crooks are in the upstairs men's bathroom. If you sneak in, you can grab the first while he's using the bathroom and ambush the second when he comes out of the first stall.

Even crooks need a bathroom break.

Alternate Stealth Approach

The easiest way to take out the bad guys in this level is to take a stealthy approach. Instead of shooting or punching through the window, just jump through it.

Action heroes can't get hurt jumping through glass.

Immediately free the theater employee and talk to him until McClane tells him to find a safe place to hide.

He seems very thankful.

Once he's free, switch to Stealth Mode and walk to the stairs on the right (if you're facing the refreshment stand). Climb the stairs to find a crook smoking. Shoot him or sneak up behind him, grab him, and break his neck.

Smoking kills.

When you're done, return to the bottom floor and then do the same thing to the bad guy practicing his moves at the top of the left stairs.

This guy needs a little more practice.

There are two more bad guys guarding the hall behind the upstairs door and two in the upstairs bathroom. You can take them out if you want or ignore them. They'll stay out of your way. Either way, return downstairs when you're done.

Dead or alive, it's up to you.

Return downstairs and jump over the counter of the refreshment stand. As you approach the door inside the concession area, you hear a crook talking on the phone and breaking into a cash register. Switch to Stealth Mode, enter the room and take him out by grabbing him and breaking his neck.

Say goodnight.

Item!

When you kill him, he drops an Armor Vest. Pick this up to get 100 armor points.

It's almost like having two lives.

When you're done, switch to dual 9mm pistols and make sure you're still in Stealth Mode. Exit quietly through the back door and you'll see three criminals playing cards.

These guys are about to be dealt a bad hand.

Don't try to grab one of them because the others will still shoot at you. Instead, open fire on them while you're still in Stealth Mode. You should be able to take them all out before they can return a single shot.

All three down.

Once they're gone, walk to the double doors on the left (when facing away from the lobby). When they open, you'll see a smoke-filled room. Without entering the room, take out the crook in the corner to your left.

Level 3: The Chinese Cinema

Take him first, he's got a submachine gun.

Make sure dual 9mm pistols are still selected and enter the room. Turn immediately to your right to find three crooks armed and ready. Shoot them all quickly.

If you're careful, you can kill all three without reloading.

Grab the submachine gun from the corner, jump over the boxes, and grab the ammo from the dead crooks. Exit through the double doors to finish this section.

Follow the doors to Part Two.

Chinese Cinema: Part Two

OBJECTIVES

* Avoid civilian casualties.

* Track down the stolen art.

* Free the remaining employees.

You start in an area overlooking a movie screen. In front of you, some crooks patrol the front of the theater.

This won't be easy.

Item!

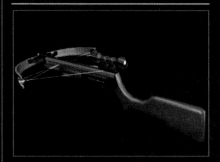

This crossbow helps if you like to be stealthy. If you don't, stick to another weapon.

Who left this lying around?

Item!

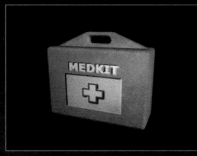

A medkit is in the opening area. Considering the danger in this level, you'll need it later.

There are a lot of bad guys to contend with on this level, so stay sharp. To use the direct approach, stay in the entrance area and shoot the two guards when they cross in front of your view.

Clean them out with your submachine gun.

Wait for the other crooks to come to you. Don't venture out too far or the crooks in the balcony will shoot at you.

The balcony snipers are your biggest threat.

TIP!

If you run low on ammo, let the guards run toward you in the entranceway. Kill them when they're inside, then grab their ammo without getting hit by a sniper.

When the crooks stop coming, venture out and shoot the balcony snipers one at a time with your 9mm Pistols. This is tricky, so let the auto-target help.

Alternate Stealth Approach

The balcony snipers are a major problem, but there's one good way to get rid of them. When you start this section, switch to Stealth Mode and watch the two guards as they cross in front of the walkway. Crouch down and follow the one on the right when he walks away.

Stay quiet and crouched.

Climb the stairs out of the entranceway, following the crook to the right for a few feet, then make a right and go up the stairs. Stay low and crawl to the back of the theater.

Stay in Stealth Mode.

When you get to the back of the theater, slide behind the back row until you get to the middle of the row. From a crouch, zoom in on the crook in the right balcony using the left trigger, and shoot him in the head.

It takes a moment for the arrow to get there.

Do the same thing to the crook on the left balcony, then crawl to the left side of the back row. Edge out into the aisle to see two crooks down below. Take them out with your crossbow.

You can get these guys, too.

Crawl down the aisle until you see a guard walking along the bottom of the movie screen and another at the bottom of the theater. Eliminate them both.

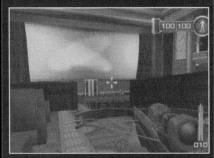

Two more stealth kills.

This leaves you with two guards near the lower exit doors. Take them out any way you like.

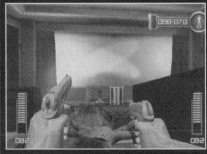

Don't forget these guys.

When the crooks are dead, find a way upstairs. Look for the *Galaxy Thief III* banner hanging on the upper level of the theater.

This banner doesn't look very secure.

Use your left trigger to target the banner's right support. Shoot it, and one end of the banner falls to the floor.

Shoot here and you're set.

Reload your best weapons. Climb up the banner by walking toward it and pushing the left joystick.

It's just like climbing a ladder.

When you reach the top, you'll see two crooks at the back of the theater. Dispatch them and pick up their submachine guns.

Short bursts of submachine gun fire finish off these guys.

Exit through the door on the right (when facing the rear of the theater). When you enter the hall, turn left. A door is on the right with crooks talking inside.

The crooks are behind the door.

Open the door and fire. You should be able to take them down without getting hit.

Make your attack quick.

Alternate Stealth Approach

An easier way to eliminate these guys is to switch to Stealth Mode when you see the door, hide against the wall, and wait until they come out of the hall.

They won't see you here.

They'll walk right by you. You can eliminate them from behind, or grab one of them from behind and take him out, then shoot the other.

Shoot them in the back.

After you eliminate the two crooks, head through the hall they came from and stop before you get to the door at the end. Be ready to fight; there's trouble on the other side.

Switch to dual submachine guns and make sure they're loaded.

Open the door and kill the guy guarding the door. Another crook makes a run for one of the doors. Don't kill him yet.

Get this guy first.

When he opens the door, unleash your fire on the crook inside the room. He's the one that will kill the hostages. When he's gone, nail the guy on the outside and the other guy on the inside.

Take the hostage guard first, then get the other two.

TIP!

The three hostages are in the room's far right corner. Don't hit them when you burst into the room.

Talk to the employees and they'll tell you that there's still one more hostage.

Save three hostages at once.

Item!

A medkit is on one of the desks. Grab it and check your current health level. If it's low, heal yourself now.

Right out in the open.

Go through the door closest to the water cooler, then through the door ahead. Climb the stairs and go through the door into the projection room.

Projection room entrance

A crook is holding the projectionist hostage. Shoot him in the back or sneak up to him in Stealth Mode and arrest him. Don't shoot the projectionist.

He's a weird one.

On the left wall (while facing the movie screen) is a switch that turns on the power to the organ. Use the action button to activate it.

Switch this on, then head downstairs.

Go out the other door, and down some stairs. When you're in the red-carpeted hall, walk through the double doors across from the *T-Rex* display, and down the stairs to your right.

Good movie.

At the base of the stairs, walk straight to another set of double doors and down an inclined hallway to an exit. Turn right to see another door. Open it.

Take the right door first.

Two crooks are in front of you. Eliminate them and step into the hallway before the guys on stage get you. Try again to see if you can get an easy shot at the guys on stage. If not, step into the hall.

It's better to fight here.

Go through the exit, then through the next door, and down some stairs to the organ. A switch is on the organ's side. Use the action button to activate it.

Organ switch.

Turn the switch and jump to the organ's top. It rises and takes you to the bottom of the movie screen.

Free ride.

At the top, you encounter the two crooks from the stage (if you didn't take them out earlier). Take them out and walk to the movie screen's right side.

On-screen action.

Item!

As you walk around the right side of the movie screen, you stumble across a medkit.

Just in time.

You enter a large backstage area. Go to the wall across from the movie screen to see a fake brick wall held up by wires.

Hey, this isn't real.

Walk to the top of the catwalk overhead and shoot the top of the pulleys holding the wires. The weights fall and the fake wall rises to reveal a hidden door.

Shoot the pulleys and the wall rises.

Walk through the door to come to another door. Switch to double submachine guns, or your best weapon, and go through.

The crooks are waiting for you.

When you enter the room, you'll encounter three crooks. There's one ahead of you and one on each side. Eliminate them and exit through the other door.

What is it with John McClane and vents?

Crouch and use your gun or your fists to bust open the vent. Climb inside and exit the level.

Three more down.

The door at the passage's end is locked, but if you take a right into the small room on the side, McClane comments about the small vent on the floor.

On to the subway.

Level 4:
The LA Subway

LA Subway: Part One

The chase for the stolen art takes John McClane below the streets of LA. It's dark and smelly.

Time to get dirty.

OBJECTIVES

* Collect evidence of paintings transported through the sewers.

* Locate a laptop used by the mercenaries to communicate.

* Rescue subway worker hostages.

* Avoid civilian casualties.

Start in the vents leading to the sewer. Duck and crawl forward until you drop into a vent. Punch out the grating in front of you.

Use your fists if you don't want to waste a bullet.

Crawl out of the vent to a large underground sewer area. Walk forward and ask the bums if they've seen anything strange.

Not much useful information from this guy.

A bum is warming up by a fire on the sewer's right hand side; talk to him. Across from him toward the center of the sewer is a sleeping bum. It's okay to wake him up.

These guys don't want to be bothered.

Item!

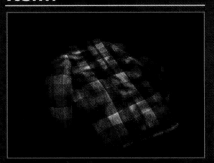

Ahead of the sleeping bum is a blue jacket with a hat on it. Grab the hobo disguise, go to your inventory menu, and activate it to put it on. It helps you blend in down here.

It may stink, but it works.

Holster your weapons and switch to Stealth Mode. Walk forward and talk to the bum on the couch. If you are not disguised and unarmed, mercenaries spot you.

Zero channels and nothing's on.

Stay in Stealth Mode and walk up to the mercenaries. Use your pistol to take them out.

Break up this meeting.

TIP!

Watch your ammo while taking out the three mercenaries in the sewer. If you're not careful, you'll run out at a bad time.

Alternate Stealth Path

To take these guys out the easy way, sneak up behind the leader (the guy in the ball cap). You can easily arrest all three and take their weapons.

They won't like it, but they'll give up if you have the leader.

Use the action button to open the rusty gate at the sewer's end and prepare for the more dangerous part of this level.

VENDETTA

Into the subway.

Walk forward until you reach a room with a locked door and a rusty vent cover. Two mercenaries are talking. When they're done, crouch, punch the cover off the vent, and crawl inside.

More vents.

As you crawl through the vents, a subway train goes by. That's a hint to watch where you walk. Take a right turn, and you're at the vent overlooking a mercenary. Shoot him.

Take him down before he spots you.

Item!

The first mercenary drops the first painting piece. Don't leave this area without having it in your inventory. It's hard to go back.

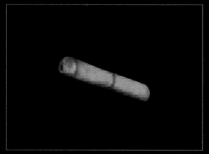

One of three.

When the first mercenary is dead, jump from the vent and turn right. In a room up the short stairway is another bad guy. Take him out with a shot in the back.

Shoot him while his back is turned.

Item!

Both of the mercenaries carry night vision goggles. You need a pair to navigate the next section safely.

Now you can see in the dark.

Item!

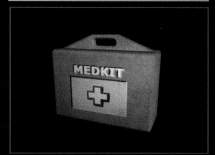

A medkit lies between the two large orange generators. It's been easy so far, but things get dangerous later.

Ah, first aid.

Put on the night vision goggles to get used to the view. They're easier to use when you're in a darkened area.

It's not easy seeing green.

Stand at the entrance to the subway tunnel and watch the trains go by. Get a feel for their speed and frequency.

This guy jumped a little early.

When you're ready, jump into the tunnel immediately after a train passes. Take a quick right and run down the tracks until you see an alcove on your right side. Jump into the alcove for safety.

A safe haven is on your right.

Continue to go from alcove to alcove in between oncoming trains. You can also jump into the maintenance holes, but you'll need to quickly drop to the ground to be safe (double tap ⇩ to crouch).

Watching a train go over your head is a rush.

TIP!

You can safely run and hide in every other alcove along the tracks. You can skip one, but don't skip two in a single run. You'll never make it.

When you reach the alcove where you hear one of the mercenaries whistling, take off your night vision goggles. As soon as a train passes, bust around the corner and take out the three mercenaries on the platform to your right.

They were waiting for a train.

Alternate Stealth Path

If you leave your night vision goggles on, you'll see a back exit in the alcove. Take this around the corner to sneak up on the mercenaries. Take off your night vision goggles before going through the door.

Sneaky, very sneaky.

Either shoot the first two in the back or quietly break their necks by grabbing them and using the attack button with no weapons armed. Shoot the third mercenary.

Amateur chiropractor at work.

When the mercenaries on your side of the tracks are dead, the bad guys on the other side of the tracks spot you. Run behind the two orange generators on the platform where you killed the two mercenaries; get between the generators and the wall.

Hide here. You'll have an easier time taking out the others.

TIP!

You don't have to shoot all the bad guys—they may try to run to you, and the subway trains will do your work for you.

From behind the generators, you can get the bad guys on the other side. Target the guy on the minigun first (on the left side of the other platform); he's your biggest threat.

Don't let the minigunner survive long, or you'll regret it.

Now carefully cross both tracks. Check all the mercenaries' bodies for weapons. A hand grenade pack is on one of them.

Daddy's girl is in big trouble.

Item!

One hand grenade pack is on a dead mercenary. Another is on the narrow walkway leading into the subway tunnel you came from. Go to the end to find the goodies.

Follow this path to the end to grab the extra grenades.

Head onto the platform with the minigun. Immediately use the action button to take control of the weapon. Some mercenaries run from the other side. Take them out with the minigun.

Easy, thanks to the minigun.

Item!

Another medkit is atop a crate behind the minigun. Now's a good time to check your health levels.

Feeling okay?

You can't open the door at the back of the platform.

It's stuck.

Activate the minigun and spin it around until it's aimed at the door. Fire into the rusty door to shoot it open.

Knock, knock.

TIP!

You can use one of your grenades to open the door. This is a good way to get used to them.

Head down the stairs to a room with an opening to the sewer pipes. A mercenary is standing to the right of the sewer pipe. Take him out.

Don't let this guy surprise you.

If the cover is blocking the opening to the sewer, you forgot to grab the first painting piece where you first entered the subway tunnel. Go get it. Otherwise, head down the tunnel to exit this section.

Down the rabbit hole.

Level 4:
The LA Subway

LA Subway: Part Two

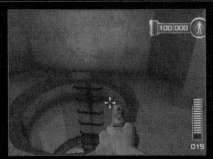

Down even deeper.

Item!

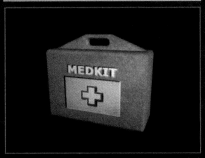

A medkit is on the ground on the lower floor. Grab it and check your health to see if you need it now.

Hey, that pipe looks open!

OBJECTIVES

* **Collect two more painting fragments.**

* **Locate a laptop used by the mercenaries to communicate.**

* **Rescue subway worker hostages.**

* **Avoid civilian casualties.**

You start in the sewers. Go through the unlocked sewer gate. Go to the next open section and take a right through the unlocked sewer gate.

Don't worry about getting lost, there's only one path.

At the end of this passage is a sewer entrance; drop down it to the floor.

Crouch and crawl through the open pipe until you hear some mercenaries talking. Don't venture too far forward or they'll spot you. When they're done talking, crawl out of the tunnel and jump out of the pit.

Get out of this pit as quickly as possible.

Four mercenaries are in this area: One on the ground, one on top of the scaffolding, and one on each platform. The safest way to fight them is to run under the platform facing the pipe you just jumped out of.

Make sure your back is covered.

From underneath this platform, you can take out the guy on the ground, the guy on the other platform, and the guy on the scaffolding.

Keep shooting.

When they're dead, back away from the platform and take out the mercenary who was above you. Pick up the ammo.

Last man standing.

Look for the ladder to the top of the scaffolding. Climb it and jump to the platform with the open entrance leading to stairs.

Use the auto-jump to clear the gap.

Climb the stairs, and a mercenary jumps out from your right. Eliminate him, then shoot the mercenary hiding in the far left corner.

You can hardly see him, but he's hiding in the shadows.

Jump the turnstiles and head into the big room that's under construction. Go into the room on the left.

Someone's doing a lot of work around here.

Item!

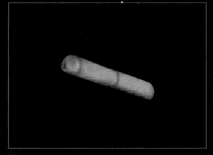

The second painting piece is on the floor next to the door. One more to go.

Two of three.

In the next room, a mercenary is talking into a laptop. Let him finish his conversation, then kill or arrest him. Use your action button to talk with Frontier in the laptop.

Web conferencing rules!

Item!

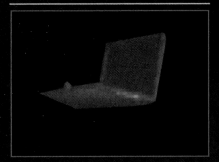

When you finish talking with Frontier, take the laptop.

Exit the laptop room, go to the large unfinished room you came from, and turn left. Switch to Stealth Mode to see two mercenaries talking to construction worker hostages.

Don't shoot the hostages.

Take out the guy closest to the hostages first, then nail his buddy standing to the left.

Two down.

Talk with the hostages and continue to the next subway platform area. Head down the short flight of stairs and you're there.

Subway platform, this way.

In the subway area, you encounter four mercenaries—two on the near platform, one on the scaffolding, and one in the dark corner of the other platform. Eliminate them all.

Don't forget the guy on top.

There's a crane holding a large pipe that seems perfect for getting you to the other side. When you jump inside and hit the action button, you'll realize you need power.

Where's the juice?

A cable leads from the crane to where you came from. Use the sandbags at the far end of the pipe to jump onto the platform.

Think of them as jump pads.

Follow the cable to the room containing the hostages to find a portable generator. It needs a key to start.

You'll need a key first.

Item!

You'll find the generator key in a blue toolbox outside the laptop room.

Just what the doctor ordered.

Stand next to the generator, and use your inventory and action button to choose the generator key. This starts the generator.

49

Purrs like a kitten.

Run to the subway platform area and jump into the crane driver's seat. When you hit the action button (⇩), you'll have power. Use the right stick to control the boom left and right, and pull down on the left joystick to rotate the pipe.

You could do this for a living.

Rotate the pipe until it's pointing at both subway platforms. Turn the crane until it's at an even distance between the two.

This ought to do it.

Use the sandbags to jump onto the platform, then jump into the pipe, run to the other side, and jump out on the other platform.

You've made it.

Open the emergency exit doors and walk into the short hallway. At the end, a mercenary is on the left. Take him out.

Item!

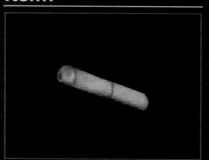

The third painting piece is here. Now you've got all the pieces.

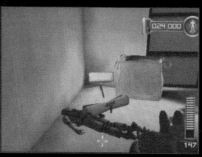

With a little restoration, it'll be as good as new.

Go through the door to see a ladder leading to a sewer drain. Climb up the ladder. Von Laben is at the top.

Him again.

Talk with Von Laben, then walk with him into the sewer. Use your action button on the door and Von Laben opens it for you.

He'll get the door.

It's easy to get lost in the sewer system. Follow the map, and keep your night vision goggles on and your weapon up so the auto-target feature can pick up bad guys you can't see.

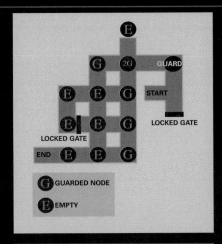

What a wuss.

Use the auto-jump to leap across the gap, then turn the valve to shut off the storm drain. He reluctantly follows you when it's safe.

After you make it across all three gaps, you reach a door that only Von Laben can open. When he does, you enter a small room. Use the action button on the valve in there to exit the level.

Maybe this wasn't such a good idea.

Watch out for guys far ahead of you.

When you reach the end of the path, Von Laben runs ahead of you and stands at the edge of some storm drains. He refuses to go across until the water stops.

Don't stress the jump, you can make it.

Level 5:
Century City Police Department

Century City Police Department: Part One

OBJECTIVES

* Avoid non-hostile casualties.
* Rescue Thornberg.

You start in the police department parking garage. Go to the ramp leading to the right. When you turn the corner, there are four mercenaries. Take them out.

Cop killers.

Grab their ammo and load up with dual submachine guns or dual 9mm pistols. Save ammo; you'll need it later.

Loaded and ready.

Continue walking through the police parking garage. Don't use the elevator. It drops you into a dangerous situation. Continue your way down on foot.

Skip the elevator.

When you reach the next ramp to the right, you'll hear mercenaries talking. Take them out from a distance with a few shots in the back.

Cleaning house.

Alternate Stealth Approach

You can also arrest all of the mercenaries if you sneak up behind the leader (the guy wearing the ball cap in the back of the group). This is easier than shooting them all, and it saves bullets and health.

They'll do what you say.

After you take out the four mercenaries on that level, proceed to the next downward ramp. Mercenaries are attaching proximity grenades to a wall.

Hey, that's police property.

Take them out quickly, then spin to your right. On the lower level near the two police cars are two more mercenaries. Take them out, too.

Get all five.

TIP!

Don't venture down anywhere in front of the two police cars. If you do, a mercenary in the nearby security office kills his hostage.

When the five mercenaries on this level are dead, switch to Stealth Mode and sneak behind the farthest police car. When you're there, target the left window of the security office and take out the mercenary inside.

Your auto-targeting picks him up.

Alternate Stealth Path

Sneak into the security office in Stealth Mode and grab the mercenary. When you have him, either arrest him or finish him off.

He's not watching the door.

Item!

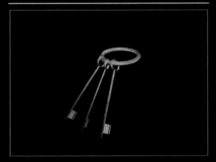

After you take out the mercenary, go into the security office and talk with the wounded cop. Talk with him long enough and he hands you the armory key. You'll be glad to have this later on.

This will come in handy.

A switch is on the wall for the security door. Use the action button to turn it until the switch points to "open."

Flip the switch.

Item!

Open the locker behind the wounded cop to find a medkit. Hopefully, you don't need it yet, because things get harder from this point on.

Kill the mercenary under the stairs.

Go to the elevator area; the security door is not open. Pick up the ammo. Shoot the proximity mine on the wall below the security camera. Watch for these later on.

Shoot this before it blows up on you.

Go through the opened security door, then through a corridor to a door. Some police officers are under fire, but you can't save them.

Sorry, there's nothing you can do.

Open the door and immediately start running. Stay to the right, using the pillars to block your enemies' line of fire. Stay along the outside until you see a set of stairs leading to a locked gate.

Make a dash for the gate.

TIP!

You can shoot all the mercenaries from the ground level if you're patient and a good shot, but it's easier to take them out from the upstairs level. Watch out for grenades while on the ground.

As you run to the locked gate, you'll see a padlock keeping it closed. Shoot the padlock and step inside the gate. Hide behind the wall at the foot of the stairs.

If you don't hit the lock quickly, the mercenaries will chew you up.

53

Climb the stairs and take out the two mercenaries at the top. Head down the stairs until you're protected from enemy fire.

Start with the two mercenaries on the stairs.

Return to the stairs and take out the two mercenaries in the balconies to your right. Watch for crossfire from your left.

Your auto-target picks up these guys.

Begin taking out the mercenaries on the other side. Drop out of view before you need to reload, and stay at the top of the stairs. When you kill the last one, a slow motion death sequence plays.

Be patient and watch your health.

After the death sequence, make your way around the top floor. After the second balcony, you'll see the red flash of a proximity grenade. Shoot it from a safe distance.

This could be deadly.

TIP!

You can safely run past proximity mines if you move at full speed. It's risky, but quicker than shooting each one.

Continue until you reach the opening of a straight passageway. A hidden mercenary shouts at you and starts shooting. Take him out, but don't walk forward.

Where was this guy hiding?

Sprint across the narrow passage. Don't go slowly; there's a proximity mine behind the pillar at the entrance.

Keep moving.

When you cross the narrow passage, Gruber flies in on a helicopter and exchanges words with you. Keep running to stay away from his minigun. The last proximity mine is on the pillar next to one of the balconies on your left.

The helicopter minigun is deadly.

TIP!

You can fight the helicopter, but you can't destroy it. A clip's worth of submachine gun bullets sends Gruber and his helicopter flying, though.

Item!

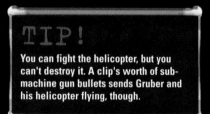

As you run around the top floor, you'll see a passage to your right that leads to double glass doors. Run past it to the last balcony and get the medkit.

It always pays to explore.

Return to the glass double doors and walk through them. Two mercenaries are on your left. Take them out.

Done and done.

Follow the passage until you see a plant in the corner. Switch to Stealth Mode and sneak behind the plant. A mercenary is laying out proximity mines. Don't shoot him. Instead, shoot the nearest proximity mine to trigger a chain reaction that kills him and sets off all his bombs.

An unfortunate chain of events.

Continue forward until you see a door and two windows on your left. Two mercenaries are shooting out of the outside windows. Take them out from behind.

Surprise.

> **TIP!**
>
> Hit the action button on the projector to learn about someone you'll soon meet.

Continue through the double doors and walk up the staircase, where there's a wounded cop. Talk with him.

He'll be okay.

Switch to Stealth Mode and enter the room just beyond the cop. Sneak around and grab the mercenary closest to you. When you have him hostage, arrest the others, then arrest or kill him.

Another successful takedown.

> **TIP!**
>
> Don't take these guys down by force or surprise attack them through the window. There's one mercenary hiding out of view who will quickly take down Thornberg.

Talk to Thornberg to end the level.

Sleazeball.

Level 5:
Century City Police Department

Century City Police Department: Part Two

OBJECTIVES

* **Avoid non-hostile casualties.**

* **Rescue Von Laben.**

* **Rescue Captain Al.**

* **Get communications back online.**

* **Rescue Lucy.**

You start where you left off, talking with Thornberg. But now you've got a lot more to do.

What are you looking at?

Item!

Go to the right corner of the room to find a medkit. Grab it.

Walk out the other door in the room (across from Thornberg) to find another set of double doors leading into a big room. It's empty, but there's danger outside.

It's quiet, too quiet.

As you enter the room, Gruber's helicopter reappears and shoots at you through the windows. Sprint out of the way and toward the double doors at the room's far end.

Run!

As you approach the double doors, you'll hear a proximity mine and McClane comments on it. Back up and let the mine take out the door and the mercenary behind it.

Kaboom.

Two more mercenaries are in the room behind the dead one. Take them out and enter the room.

Later, guys.

Go out through the double doors, down the stairs, and follow the hallway until you see a room with two mercenaries beating up Captain Al. Shoot them both through the glass.

Don't let them pummel Al.

Talk with Captain Powell, then follow him to your next battle. In the first hallway (when you see windows to a large office), a mercenary will surprise attack you. Eliminate him, then run to your left to take out another would-be attacker.

He smells bacon.

Return to the large office with all the windows to find three mercenaries talking around a computer in the back of the office. Shoot them from the inside, or blast them through the window from the hallway.

1-2-3, it's easy.

Item!

After the mercenaries are dead, grab the medkit on the desk they were surrounding. Check your health.

They won't need this anymore.

Run down the stairs. A bad guy is at the bottom. Eliminate him and turn the corner to see two archways. Take the first one.

Use the arch on the right.

At the bottom of this set of stairs, you'll fight two mercenaries. Take care of them quickly and proceed to their location.

They don't have the armory key.

If you grabbed the armory key from the wounded security officer, you can walk in. Continue into the armory.

Item!

On the counter of the armory is the SWAT vest. Pick it up and your armor rating jumps to 100.

57

You'll feel safer.

Item!

Open the door and walk behind the counter to see two storage lockers. The right one contains a combat shotgun. This is a handy weapon to use in close-quarters combat.

Nice, very nice.

Item!

On the desk behind the counter is a medkit. With all this great stuff, you know there's trouble coming soon.

Another medkit…uh, oh.

Head out of the armory, up the stairs, and into the second archway. You can enter the row of three observation rooms, but you won't be able to save the prisoners.

Skip these if you want.

At the end of the hall take a quick left, and you'll see a mercenary. Kill him and look into the window of the last observation room to see Lucy and Von Laben.

Door's locked.

Before you rescue Lucy, take the first hall-way to the left and kill all the mercenaries that are in or nearby the interview rooms.

That's not standard police procedure.

Return to the I.D. Parade Room and use the action button on the intercom to talk to Lucy. When she prompts you, shoot the glass.

Nope, it's bulletproof.

Wait until she throws the chair, then shoot the part of the glass that buckles. Aim for the smudge the chair made on the previous throw. If you time it correctly, the glass shatters.

That'll do it.

Item!

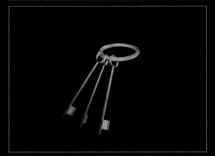

Continue to talk with Lucy and Von Laben to learn more about what's happening. She gives you the holding cell keys.

Time to free some prisoners.

Round the next corner to reach barred doors that were previously locked. Go through the doors, down the stairs, and into the holding cells.

You can talk to all of the inmates, but you need to approach Herbert Dowd and Nitric. Herbert is the white guy with glasses, and Nitric is Hispanic with bad skin.

Herbert Dowd.

Talk to both of them until you get to a verbal clue that is the equivalent of "I'm going to let you out." Release both prisoners.

Nitric.

TIP!

You can follow both prisoners if you want, but you only need to follow Nitric. Dowd will fix the communications; release him first. Nitric won't act until he's done.

Follow Nitric to the bomb and go behind the counter when he instructs you. He disarms the bomb and this section ends.

Maybe you shouldn't trust this guy.

Level 5: Century City Police Department

Century City Police Department: Part Three

OBJECTIVES

* Avoid non-hostile casualties.

* Obtain the evidence suitcase.

From your spot in the police station room, load your double submachine guns. Run through the doors with the recently disarmed bombs.

It looks dangerous outside.

When you exit, three mercenaries attack you. Take them down quickly.

It is dangerous outside.

Alternate Path

Shoot the police car a couple of times and it explodes. All three mercenaries are taken out by the wreckage.

Car troubles.

You are continually attacked from here on out, so make sure your gun is loaded and your health is full. You should have several medkits stored.

They're everywhere.

After you kill the first three mercenaries at the door, you see two more to the right. The one farther back holds the evidence suitcase. You'll know it because he dies with a slo-mo death animation.

That's the suitcase you're looking for.

When you get the suitcase, clear the entire area of mercenaries. There are as many as 20, so be prepared for intense action.

Here are more bad guys than you've faced so far.

TIP!

Use short, controlled bursts with your dual submachine guns. You have ammo from the dead mercenaries, but you don't want to reload while someone is shooting at you.

When you kill the final mercenary (there is another death sequence), Gruber's helicopter lands and the level ends.

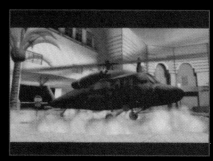

Helicopters always bring trouble.

Level 6:
Hollywood Film Studio

Hollywood Film Studio: Part One

Don't waste time in front of the gate; the sniper will make you pay.

OBJECTIVES

* **Avoid non-hostile casualties.**

* **Find Lucy McClane.**

* **Find the paintings.**

* **Support the SWAT team.**

You start in the driveway of a Hollywood movie studio. Run to the road's end to see a closed gate in front of you and a SWAT trooper guarding the entrance.

Welcome to the party, pal.

When you go through the gate, you'll see several injured SWAT officers. Talk with them, then go behind them to the right.

He won't let you pass.

Ignore the SWAT trooper and walk to the right of the guard post. The gate is locked; shoot the lock with your pistol and walk through.

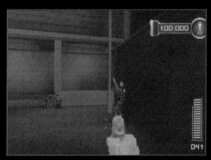

It's only a flesh wound.

When you turn the corner, you'll see another group of SWAT troops. A sniper shoots one of them. If you are nearby when this happens, grab his gun.

TIP!

If you can't grab the shotgun after the SWAT trooper dies, wait until you hear another sniper shot, then get the shotgun.

Item!

Talk with the SWAT team leader (the one without a helmet) until he asks you to take care of the sniper and gives you the stage swipe pass.

Back stage pass!

Return the way you came and go past the entrance gate toward Stage 2.

61

Trouble in Stage 2.

Go around the corner to your right, and before you turn the second corner, inch out to the side until you see an elevated walkway. Aim your crosshairs at the walkway, then slide out sideways. Take out the single shooter in the walkway.

He's not easy to hit.

Face the large sliding studio door in Stealth Mode and use the action button to open it. Without moving, switch to Action Mode and shoot the mercenary on the lift crane.

Get him immediately, so he won't harass you from above.

Take out a mercenary on the ground level and another on the catwalk above the movie set.

Make him part of the scenery.

Climb the ladder to the top of the sci-fi set, switch to Stealth Mode, and drop into a hole in the far left corner. When you do, you'll hear a couple of guys talking, and one mercenary leaves. Let him go before you attack.

Don't take them all on at once.

Move into the open, where you can get a clean shot at the guy in the hat, and switch into Action Mode. Take him out when your crosshairs turn red, then take out the guy next to him. The mercenary that departed runs around the corner, followed by another.

Stay put and take them all out.

TIP!

Use a short, controlled burst of fire on the mercenary in the hat who's guarding the hostages. If you hold the trigger, you'll nail a hostage.

Alternate Approach

If you don't want to risk taking out a hostage, sneak up on the mercenary who's wearing a hat, and grab him. Drag him to the other three mercenaries and arrest them all.

It's slower, but much safer.

Item!

Talk to the hostage on the far left and eventually he gives you the executive key. This helps you get through the upstairs areas.

This guy needs a new agent.

Work your way through the area under the set (where the third mercenary came from) until you reach a door leading out. Take the stairs to the left and you'll be back where you started.

It looks like a maze, but it's impossible to get lost.

Item!

Take a sharp right before you exit the under-set maze to find a short path that leads to a medkit.

Almost forgot this one.

Jump on the lift crane and use the action button on the control pad in the basket. This takes you to the catwalk above the sci-fi set.

Going up.

Item!

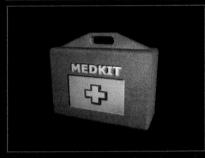

Take a right at the first junction of the catwalk to find a medkit. Use it if your health is near 50 or below. Otherwise, save it.

Must belong to a gaffer.

Exit through the door at the top of the stage to see the mercenary you killed from below. Grab his ammo. Continue until you reach another studio door. Open it to find a giant castle set.

A guard is in the middle gap between the battlements on the front of the castle. Use your assault rifle zoom to take him out. Another mercenary is hiding in the same spot on the other side of the gate.

Hit them before they spot you.

Climb down the stairs carefully, and run through the front gate. You'll see a large wooden backdrop barrier. Run around the left side and immediately turn right. Eliminate the mercenary.

Surprise!

Slide to the right to see another mercenary sneaking around the side of the wooden backdrop you came from. Take him out, too.

Make it quick.

Grab both the mercenaries' submachine guns and shoot at the castle's left interior walls. It falls apart to reveal a mercenary.

Is anything real in LA?

Shoot castle walls until you open a path to the back. Slide over one space and do the same thing to the next interior wall. Go across the castle doing this, and kill any mercenaries you uncover.

When you're done, there should be no walls between you and the back wall.

Grab the ammo from the dead mercenaries, and head to the room's back left corner, where there is a ladder. Climb it.

Climb slowly or you'll run over the other side.

When you reach the ladder's top, drop into a crouch, switch to Stealth Mode, and move along the castle's back interior wall. Slowly go to the two steps at the opposite back corner.

Be prepared to fall.

Item!

If you're a skilled jumper, you can grab a medkit by taking an immediate left and auto-jumping to the middle when you reach the ladder's top.

One tough item to get.

When you reach the far back corner, jump to the top step. Move back on the step so you have running room, switch to Action Mode, then leap to the catwalk on the other side.

You're safe now.

Climb the stairs and go through the door on the studio's back wall. A gunman is around the second corner; eliminate him. Progress through the elevated walkway to see another mercenary. Shoot him through the glass before he sees you.

Get him first.

Progress through a couple more offices and sneak up on the sniper. Take him out quickly from a distance.

That's for the dead SWAT trooper.

Pick up his sniper rifle and get ready to take down some mercenaries at a distance. Take them down with a head shot, then move to the next one. Check the map for the location and order of each target.

Aim for their heads.

TIP!

It's better to take your time and make a clean head shot than waste ammo and time on body shots. Three body shots cause the same damage as a single head shot.

After you take out the four snipers, jump off the balcony to the red inflatable crash pad.

Look out below.

Item!

When you reach the ground, head to the water tower to see the SWAT troopers surrounding the room containing the lost painting. Enter the room to pick up some blank minigun ammo. You'll need it elsewhere.

Pick up the minigun ammo, then go to the far side of the studio area (across from the water tower).

Follow this road.

You'll see a road leading to a locked gate. Take a left before the gate to see an open door. Enter to end the level.

On to Studio 3.

Level 6:
Hollywood Film Studio

Hollywood Film Studio: Part Two

OBJECTIVES

* Avoid non-hostile casualties.

* Find Lucy McClane.

You start in the stairwell outside a jungle set. Switch to your assault rifle and enter the set. Take a left and slowly make your way toward the bridge. Take out a couple of mercenaries with the auto-target.

65

If it glows red, they're as good as dead.

Run onto the bridge. It explodes and drops you into the ravine.

Don't worry, it won't hurt.

When you get to the bottom, a mercenary behind you sees you. Take care of him. When you're done, you'll see a demolition switch on a small table. Use the action button to activate it and knock a palm tree across the gap.

Timber.

Item!

In the corner behind the table is an extra medkit. Grab it and save it.

One for the road.

Use the fallen bridge as a ladder, and climb out of the ravine. When you reach the top, you'll see the palm tree that fell across the gap. Use it as a bridge, and walk to the other side.

Keep your balance.

When you hit the other side, your auto-target picks up another bad guy. Take him out. Move forward and look for another mercenary in the far left corner. Take him out, too. The sniper rifle works well.

Another one bites the dust.

You're left with two mercenaries holding some high-priced actors hostage. If you want to test your skills as a sniper, take them out from the far left side. This is risky; there's a better way.

Hope you know what you're doing.

Alternate Approach

If you grabbed the blank mini-gun ammo, run to the mini-gun facing the mercenaries and use the action button.

Are you crazy?

The minigun fires, but you're using blanks, so no one will be hurt. The mercenaries cower to the ground while the actors flee. Use your assault rifle to finish off the mercenaries.

Movie magic.

TIP!

Don't get carried away with the mini-gun. Use it until the mercenaries release the hostages, then switch to your rifle to finish them off before they fire at you.

Before you leave the jungle set, grab the ammo from the dead mercenaries.

Even dead, he's useful.

Exit the set and listen for an actress practicing in the closest trailer. There's a block under one of the tires to keep the trailer from rolling down a hill.

What's this for?

If you walk down the hill to your left, you'll realize that the gate is locked. Return to the trailer and shoot out the block from in front of the tire. Get out of the way!

The insurance company's gonna be mad.

The trailer breaks through the gate and you can run through. Stop for a second and talk with Jessie Montana, the actress.

She's not very happy.

Run toward the western set, where the helicopter is taking off. A bunch of bad guys is there. Take out the bad guys, but save ammo for the next battle.

Watch the guys on the right; they can cause you trouble.

Item!

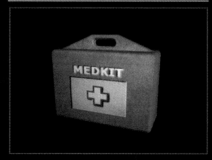

Grab the medkit in the back of the trailer before you face Nitric.

Every medkit counts at the end of this level.

Nitric comes out to fight you. He's an incredibly difficult opponent.

You should've left him rotting in the jail.

If you have hero points stored up, use them now. Hit your left trigger and ⊙ after he empties his clip in your direction.

Wait until he's done shooting before you go into Hero Mode.

When you go into Hero Mode, shoot him in the head. The assault rifle and the dual submachine guns work. If you aim right, he's done in seconds.

Aim only at his head.

TIP!

You can wound Nitric without going into Hero Mode. Aim for his head and keep moving. Attack when he reloads for your best opportunity to do damage.

When Nitric goes down, Captain Al shows up and throws you into jail for defying orders. It's going to be another tough day.

C'mon, this isn't fair.

OBJECTIVES

* Avoid non-hostile casualties.

* Escape from prison.

* Rescue the prison warden.

* Attempt to capture Nitric.

Level 7: The Sierra Correctional Facility

The Sierra Correctional Facility: Part One

You start in a prison cell talking with Nitric. Before long, he escapes, releases all the prisoners, and starts a riot. It's time to track him down.

Hard time.

Wait until the top floor guard passes by, sneak up behind him, grab him, and bring him into your cell. Use the action button to arrest him and he drops a combat shotgun.

Alternate Approach

You can hide from the guards without grabbing them if you prefer, but this isn't recommended. If you do that, you can't grab the shotgun.

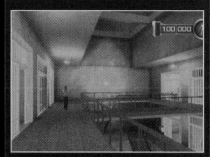

Keep an eye on the guards at all times.

Carefully venture out onto the top floor. All the doors are open, but the prisoners stay in their cells. A guard is below you.

Freedom, sort of.

Freedom, sort of.

TOP LEVEL

JAIL CELLS

| 1 START POINT | 2 | EMPTY | EMPTY | OCCUPIED |

STAIRS DOWN

STAIRS DOWN

| EMPTY | OCCUPIED | OCCUPIED | EMPTY | EMPTY | OCCUPIED |

JAIL CELLS

1 NITRIC'S CELL   2 HINT CELL

1 **Nitric's cell: Grab tuna can**
2 **Talk to learn about flammable mattress**
3 **Talk to learn about escape plan**
4 **Pick up cigarettes**

MIDDLE LEVEL

JAIL CELLS

| 7 | OCCUPIED | EMPTY | OCCUPIED | 3 | 4 |

STAIRS DOWN   STAIRS UP

STAIRS UP   STAIRS DOWN

| EMPTY | 6 | OCCUPIED | OCCUPIED | 5 | OCCUPIED |

JAIL CELLS

3 HINT CELL
4 PICK UP CIGARETTES
5 GET LIT CIGARETTE
6 LIGHT THE MATTRESS
7 HIDE HERE

5 **Get the lit cigarette**
6 **Light the mattress**
7 **Hide while the guard puts out the fire**

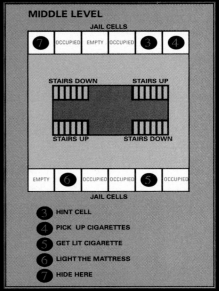

Item!

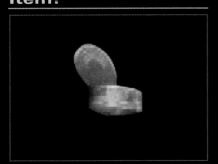

Walk to the cell to your cell's left (from the outside looking in). This was Nitric's cell 1. Inside you'll find a tuna can; keep it.

Go to the cell to the right of yours 2 and talk with the prisoner. He tells you about a room containing a flammable mattress. This gives you an idea.

Now that's a good plan.

TIP!

Watch out for the guard on the lower floor. If you're not careful, he spots you from below. If he does, jump into the closest empty cell before he counts to three.

Talk to the rest of the prisoners on the top floor, then watch for the guard on the middle floor. Sneak down the stairs behind him.

Don't let the guard spot you.

Grab him and arrest him in an empty cell, or avoid him. It's easiest to arrest him.

Sorry, buddy.

69

Go into the cell that has a prisoner lying down in it ③. He gives you an idea for your escape.

Free advice.

Item!

Go into the empty room beside the prisoner you just talked to ④ to find a pack of cigarettes on a bed. Pick them up—you can use them soon.

Who left these lying around? In prison, they're like currency.

Go across from the cell containing the prone prisoner to find another convict who wants a cigarette. Use your inventory to find the cigarettes and the action button to give him one.

You've made a prison buddy.

Item!

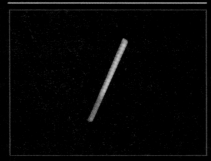

The convict lights your cigarette and you now have a lit cigarette in your inventory.

It's arson time!

Take the lit cigarette to the room containing the soiled mattress ⑥. Walk to the mattress, select the lit cigarette in your inventory, and hit the action button.

Fire, fire!

A guard runs in to extinguish the flames. Before he spots you, duck into an empty cell near the stairs leading down ⑦.

Wait here until he runs past.

Stay hidden until the guard enters the burning cell with a fire extinguisher. In Stealth Mode, sneak behind the guard, down the stairs, and into the opened guard room. Inside is a storage locker. Open it, crouch, climb inside, and close it.

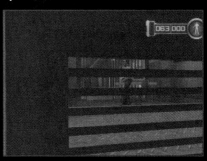

The perfect hiding place.

Wait until the guard returns to his desk. Sneak out of the locker and through the now-opened second door. As you exit, watch for the two guards carrying boxes on your right.

You've come too far to get caught now.

TIP!

If you're spotted, run for the elevator control, then into the elevator. Even if they spot you, you can escape to the roof.

Go through the door across from the guard room where another guard works at a computer. Sneak behind him and flip the lift control switch on the wall across from the door.

Keep it cool.

Go out the door to the open elevator on your left. Sneak into it, flip the switch, and head to the roof.

Your ticket out.

When you reach the roof, there's more danger. Take a right and run to the roof's far end.

This could get ugly.

A helicopter flying overhead shoots at you. Keep running. When you reach a series of skylights, run along the roof portion. Don't run across the glass.

Stay on the solid section.

Continue running and avoid the falling antenna. Eventually, there is a large explosion in the roof's far left corner. Go to the point of the explosion, where there's a hole in the roof. Jump into the hole.

Back inside.

When you drop into the prison, go to a locked door and you'll hear a prisoner say, "The whole place is gonna blow." Turn and jump into the laundry chute to end this part of the level.

Jump!

Level 7:
The Sierra Correctional Facility

The Sierra Correctional Facility: Part Two

OBJECTIVES

* **Avoid non-hostile casualties.**

* **Escape from prison.**

* **Rescue the prison warden.**

* **Attempt to capture Nitric.**

You start in the prison laundry. If you walk into the next hallway, you encounter a locked door and a dangerous gunfight. Instead, stay in the laundry room and push the laundry cart into the hall and through the door. Follow it closely to avoid gunfire.

Easy opening doors.

Go to the end of the next room and open the far left door. A wounded cop is inside. Talk with him; he needs a medkit.

Officer down.

Leave the room through the next door and take a right. At the end of the hallway is a locked gate with three prisoners running on its other side. Turn around to see a small opening on your right side (facing the direction from which you came).

Another passage.

Go through the opening and up the stairs. At the top, two prisoners look at a map on a table. If you captured the guard at the beginning of this level, use the shotgun to take them out.

No more plans for these guys.

Alternate Approach

If you avoided the guards in the first part of this level, you're unarmed. Sneak up to the first prisoner, grab him, break his neck, and take his gun. Quickly shoot the second prisoner.

The hard way.

Go down the hallway. At the exit on the far right side is an armory. Grab the 9mm from the dead cop inside.

The weapons have been cleaned out.

Item!

On the other side of the hall is a medkit on a table. Grab it, but don't use it.

The wounded cop could use this.

Item!

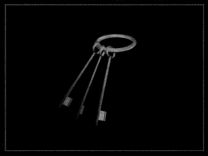

Run the way you came until you reach the wounded cop. When you're next to him, open your inventory and use the action button on the medkit to give it to him. He gives you the locker key.

He still looks bad.

Run to the armory and enter through the broken fence on the room's right side. Open the locker to find a combat shotgun.

Whoo-hoo!

Alternate Approach

If you're low on health and already have a combat shotgun, use the medkit on yourself and hope that someone else helps the guard.

You wouldn't...would you?

Step out of the armory and go left. At the hallway's end is a passage leading to the right. Follow it. At the passage's end is a door leading into a storage room.

Boxes and boxes.

Enter the room and turn right. Two prisoners think you're trying to steal their supplies; shoot them.

Exit the room and take a sharp right. You'll see a prisoner kicking a dead guard. Eliminate him. When you're done, flip the switch on the wall closest to the dead guard to open the big metal door at the room's end.

Quit kicking him.

When you open the door, make a sprint for the semi trailer in the middle of the yard. Shoot the guy in the trailer on your way there. Grab his sniper rifle, but switch back to your combat shotgun.

Keep on truckin'.

Item!

A medkit is on a crate in the back of the trailer. Check your health now.

Excellent.

Run to the metal door you opened. Turn around and kill the three prisoners in the yard to your left. Stay near the building you exited—a sniper is in the watch tower on your left.

Watch out for the sniper in the watch tower.

When the prisoners on the ground are dead, inch away from the building until you can barely see the guy in the watch tower. Zoom in on him with your sniper rifle and try for a head shot.

Take him down quickly.

Switch to Stealth Mode. Grab ammo and an assault rifle from the three prisoners you killed in the yard. Run toward the watch tower's base. Stop before you reach the entrance to the next yard.

More trouble ahead.

Sneak into the entranceway and pick off the prisoners in the two guard towers above you. This is a difficult shot, so aim carefully.

The guard in the closest tower hides next to one of the posts.

TIP!

In this prison yard, there are three guards on the left side of the open area. Don't fight them; run away. Stay in Stealth Mode whenever you move and don't let them see you. Don't shoot them either.

Take out the prisoners standing near the exercise equipment in the yard. There are at least three. The guards may get one or two, though.

Don't forget the guy hiding at the end of the yard.

Head to the end of the yard. If you're spotted, keep moving. Go into the building at the far end. You'll see glass blow out into the entranceway, followed by a huge explosion.

This can't be good.

Enter the room and crouch. Stay in Stealth Mode, switch to your sniper rifle or assault rifle, and take out the prisoners in the yard.

Take them down with head shots.

TIP!

If the prisoners spot you and start shooting, hide again. Wait until they stop shooting, switch to Stealth Mode, get into a good spot, then open fire.

Item!

Don't leave this room without picking up the medkit on the table in the corner.

Very useful.

Leave the room and head into the hallway. From the right (facing the yard) entrance into this new prison yard, you can spot the prisoner hiding in the farthest watch tower. Take him out with your sniper rifle. Another is hidden in the tower closest to the entrance.

You can barely see him, but he sees you.

Head into the prison yard and grab the ammo off the dead prisoners. Climb the ladder sitting against the left wall.

Up again.

When you reach the top, locate a hole in one of the walls. Shoot the prisoner guarding this library entrance and jump in.

He's protective of the books.

Leave the room, go upstairs, take a right, head down the hallway, and take a left. Two prisoners are talking. Kill them both, then kill the other two around the next corner.

Isn't he the guy who shared a smoke with you earlier?

Enter the elevator and head into the belly of the prison. It only gets harder from here.

Going down.

Level 7:
The Sierra Correctional Facility

The Sierra Correctional Facility: Part Three

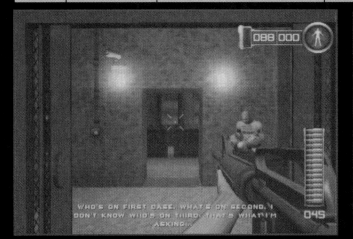

OBJECTIVES

* **Avoid non-hostile casualties.**
* **Escape from prison.**
* **Rescue the prison Warden.**
* **Attempt to capture Nitric.**
* **Acquire a SWAT vest.**

As you exit the elevator, you'll see a crazy prisoner sitting on a box. Talk with him to get a clue for opening a locked door ahead. If you don't get the clue right away, keep talking to him; he eventually gives it up.

Who's on first?

Go past the prisoner and take the first door to your right. A row of switches is inside. Follow the crazy guy's advice, turn the switches properly, and the door opens with a buzz.

Up, Down, Up, Up, Down.

Item!

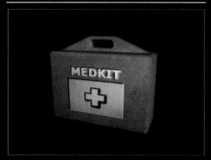

There's a medkit under the TV in the switch room. Don't leave without it.

Exit the switch room and go through the newly opened door into the area housing insane criminals. Switch to your assault rifle, go through the door at the room's far end, and slowly go through the next door.

Someone's in trouble.

Sneak around the corner and look down below the stairs. Two prisoners are holding a doctor hostage. Shoot the one closest to the doctor first, then kill the other one to earn Hero Points.

Don't hit the doctor.

Return to the holding area and enter the cell with the poster of a girl on the wall. Use your action button on the picture and the poster falls to reveal an escape tunnel. Crouch and follow the tunnel.

Oh, you beauty.

When you enter the next area, look right to see a ladder going up. Take that ladder into a vent with huge spinning fans.

This looks deadly.

One fan isn't spinning, but you can't get past it. A knob with five settings is on the front. Use your action button to turn the fan on to its first setting.

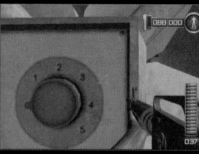

Turn it up.

The fan starts spinning slowly, pushing you back. Turn up the speed until the fan explodes and one of the blades falls off. Don't let the wind blow you into the fan behind you, and don't run into the one in front of you.

It's tricky, but you can do it.

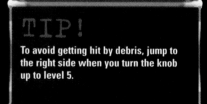

TIP!

To avoid getting hit by debris, jump to the right side when you turn the knob up to level 5.

Crouch and climb under the broken fan blade, then climb the ladder to your right. A prisoner is talking to a SWAT trooper hanging from a rope.

If you wait too long, he dies.

Now's the time to use the Hero Points you just earned. Switch into Hero Mode by holding the left trigger and hitting ⊘. Use the action button to open the vent and immediately shoot the rope that's holding up the SWAT trooper.

Even in Hero Mode, this shot must be quick.

TIP!

Don't worry about the other SWAT trooper, he's dead.

When the rope breaks, shoot the guy standing next to the SWAT trooper. Spin to the right and pick off the guy on that far side. Go to the right side of the pillars and nail two more prisoners on the other side. One more shows up on your right. Take him out, too.

You can get the first four while in Hero Mode.

TIP!

You can save the SWAT trooper in regular mode, but this is easier. Make sure to shoot the rope first.

Item!

Talk to the trooper to get a SWAT vest so you won't get shot by the SWAT team. You'll also replace the Hero Points you just used.

Ah, it was nothing.

Push the control button on the open door that the SWAT trooper is facing. It closes and opens the door behind it. The switch will explode.

Poor craftsmanship.

Climb up the stairwell in the room, then travel around the upper balcony until you reach a destroyed console and an open vent. Jump to enter the vent.

More crawling.

Climb through the vent until you drop in front of the opened door. Walk through the hallway until you see two prisoners running. Gun them down.

They saw you.

If you don't get them in time, they'll run behind some boxes and join four other convicts in a long hallway. When you get there, crouch behind a crate and take out all the prisoners with your assault rifle and sniper rifle, if necessary.

There's a lot of them.

Item!

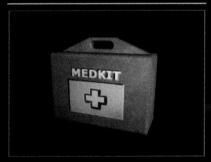

After they're dead, turn around to see a door. Open it to reveal a small room with a medkit inside.

Check your health.

Work your way through the hallway in Stealth Mode. A prisoner is behind the screen to your right. Kill him.

He thinks he's safe.

Jump through the hole in the fence at the hallway's far end. Go straight and take a quick right. Kill the prisoner there. Past him, take a right in the large hallway.

Don't let him scare you.

The hallway leads to a room filled with fighting prisoners and SWAT members. Kill the prisoners, but don't hit the SWAT troopers.

Bloody battle.

Exit through the far doors to find the SWAT team staging area. Talk to the SWAT leader (the guy without the hat) to continue. When McClane says "Look, if you find Nitric, we can all go home," you can go through the double doors.

He doesn't like guys who don't play by the rules.

Item!

You exit into a medical area. Go to the postered wall to find a medkit on the shelf to your right.

They won't need this for a while.

Continue past the large metal tanks and through the left door. Take a quick left at the hallway and kill the three prisoners at the other end of the hall.

Watch for the guy on the stairs.

Climb the stairs, take the first right, and the quick right after it. Shoot the guy standing in front of the door and the other guy around the corner.

It's the Warden's office.

Enter the Warden's office, take a quick right, and shoot the two prisoners in front of the fireplace. Get behind the desk and push it toward the fireplace.

Rearrange the office.

Item!

As you push the desk, you uncover the safe combination.

He shouldn't have left this lying around.

Item!

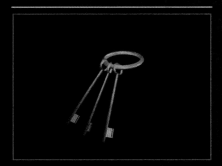

Push the desk to the fireplace and jump on top. Use the action button on the painting to reveal a safe. Use action on the safe to grab the master keys.

Ah-ha!

Leave the Warden's office and take the first hallway on the right. A bad guy is around the first corner and another is on the stairs. Climb the stairs until you reach a door. Open it and kill the prisoner inside the observation room. The prisoners are yelling below.

It's gonna get hairy.

Leave the room, go down the stairs, and open the door to a large storage room. Turn right and kill all four prisoners in a line. Walk in their direction to see another door.

There's more of them.

Go through the door to an observation window showing the five prisoners in the execution room. Go through the next door to find the room's entrance.

Loaded up?

Bust through the door and kill all five prisoners. Don't let them activate the panel at the far end of the room. When they're dead, use Ⓐ to free the Warden.

What a save!

Talk with the Warden and he shows you how to get to the roof for your final showdown with Nitric.

It's go time.

Level 7:
The Sierra Correctional Facility

The Sierra Correctional Facility: Part Four

* Avoid non-hostile casualties.

* Escape from prison.

* Attempt to capture Nitric.

Talk with the Warden, then go through the door and up the stairs on the right. Go through the door to the roof to five prisoners: One on the roof of the door you came through, one behind you on the ground, two in front of you, and one on the satellite dish base.

Don't forget the one on the roof behind you.

Item!

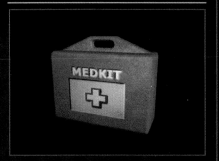

Continue to the room under the satellite dish. A handy medkit is inside.

Use it. You'll need full health in a moment.

Go through the open gate to find Nitric. Run to the right side of the helipad and up the stairs until you're almost face-to-face.

The final showdown.

Switch to Hero Mode and unload everything you have into his head. He should quickly die. If you don't have Hero Points, fight him by staying to the outside, then

shooting when he reloads. Watch for grenades; they're deadly.

Dead.

If you're not on the helipad, go to it now to end the level and get a full pardon from Captain Al.

Can he do that, legally?

Level 8: Cesar Tuna Factory

Cesar Tuna Factory: Part One

He thinks he's hidden.

OBJECTIVES

* Avoid non-hostile casualties.

* Investigate tuna factory.

* Rescue factory workers.

There are several different ways to start this level and get inside the tuna factory's front door. Choose your path by using these basic approaches. Start each one by shooting out the camera in front of you.

Don't forget to eliminate this camera.

The Direct Approach

When the level starts, run around the corner to your left and fire a clip at the mercenaries' heads. Quickly back up to where you came from, unload and take out the bad guys as they round the corner. Use the crates and the wall to your right to protect you.

The bodies will pile up.

When you're done, kill the final mercenary guarding the tuna factory entrance. He's in the room with large glass windows. Sneak up on him by crouching into the room in Stealth Mode and shooting him behind the counter.

The Silent Approach

Stay in Stealth Mode and go to the back wall, then left into the minigun room. Keep walking in Stealth Mode toward the semi trailer until you're facing the truck's grill.

Wait here for mercenary leader.

Hide along the containers and wait for the leader (the one in the hat) to walk by. When he passes you, grab him and use him to arrest the other mercenaries. You can make the guy in the guard room drop his gun before you shoot him.

Easy arrests.

81

The Minigun Approach

Stay alongside the right wall in Stealth Mode and run to the other side of the yard. (If you leave quickly, you can pass the guards while they're getting orders.) Sneak along, keeping the wall to your right.

Move quickly.

You'll reach a point where you see a minigun. Use the action button to activate it, and watch the guards pass by the canisters on the far side. When one sees you, start shooting.

> **TIP!**
> Switch to Action Mode before activating the minigun, and aim with the set of crosshairs.

You've been spotted.

The others will come running from either side of the shack's door. Clean them out quickly. Watch for guys on both sides.

It's easy when they come from the sides.

When you kill all the mercenaries in the yard, the guard in the guard room comes out his front door. Shoot him, too. A slow motion death sequence indicates that you're done.

The Direct Minigun Approach

You also can reach the minigun by turning the corner, shooting one of the mercenaries, sprinting ahead, and turning left when you reach the back wall. Run to the minigun and begin firing.

Pause here for a second.

If you time your run carefully (add a second or two of pause time), the mercenaries will follow you toward the yard's back corner then try to attack you from the front when you're on the minigun. Line up your sights against the door's left side and they'll walk right into your fire without ever firing back.

Like shooting ducks in a row.

If you get to the gun too early, they come at you from two different directions; if you wait too long, they hit you from the side door. When you're done, the last mercenary comes out of the tuna factory door.

You can attack from here without ever getting hit.

The Over-the-Top Approach

Sneak around the far right side until you reach a point where the wall forces you to make your first left turn. Take another left turn at the first opportunity to find a crate that you can jump up on.

This looks useful.

From that crate, jump onto another set of crates, then turn right to see the tops of the other containers in the yard. Leap along these using the auto-jump until you get to the top of the semi-trailer.

Don't get spotted by the guards on the ground.

This is the most difficult path into the tuna factory. Avoid it unless all the guards are dead or if you really want to test your skills.

From the top of the semi, jump onto the awning above the building to a walkway and door on the next building. This allows you to play through this section of the map in a different order than you usually would.

The back door.

Item!

Before you enter the tuna factory, go to the outside wall across from the drivers' door of the semi to see a large metal door. Open it, and grab the hand grenades inside.

Keep them for emergencies.

Return to the entrance room (the one with the glass windows) and go through the door inside. You'll enter another room with a door that leads to a hallway. Take the first left, and fire a bullet into the open area to draw out the three hiding mercenaries.

Lure them into the open and take them out.

When the three mercenaries are dead, go forward, take a left and exit through the door at the far end of the hall. You're in a loading area. Use the wall switch to open the large metal door.

Outside again.

When you step through the door, you'll hear two crooks taking target practice at a factory worker. Run toward the factory worker, take a quick left, and gun them both down.

Shoot quickly or they kill the hostage.

Alternate Approach

Push the trash bin between the factory worker and the shooters to protect him and draw them to you. It is difficult to get the trash bin in the correct spot.

Saved by garbage.

83

PRIMA'S OFFICIAL STRATEGY GUIDE

Item!

After you talk to the rescued factory worker, push the trash bin against the crates he was standing beside, jump onto the trash bin, then onto the crates. Crouch and squeeze into the doorway behind the crates to find a medkit.

There it is.

Go through the blue door next to where the crooks were standing and enter a hallway. Take the blue door at the hall's end, climb the stairs, and take a left at the top.

Someone really needs to clean up this room.

In the room, two doors are next to each other. Take the one on the right to find a mercenary and two hostages. Carefully take out the mercenary with a short, controlled burst of gunfire.

Don't hit the hostages.

Alternate Approach

Go into the bathroom at the top of the stairs, crawl through the vent, and shoot the mercenary with your 9mm from inside.

Don't use an automatic weapon; you might hit the hostages.

After you kill the guy holding the hostages, two other mercenaries come out of the other room and shoot at you. Take them out from inside the room containing the hostages.

Get them when they enter the doorway.

Alternate Approach

If you used the Over-the-Top approach to start this level, take out the guy guarding the hostages

from outside. Watch for the two guys coming from the other room, and go back to rescue the hostage who the bad guys are using for target practice.

You can play this part of the level backwards.

Item!

Once you've rescued the hostages, talk to the one on your right (while facing the windows) to get the gantry keys.

Thanks!

Go into the room next door (a security monitor is inside), and locate a door on a walkway outside the window. Jump through the window, and go through the door to exit the level.

The fun's just beginning.

Level 8:
Cesar Tuna Factory

Cesar Tuna Factory: Part Two

Time your jumps and use the two moving crates to make it to the upper level on the other end. Use auto-jump and lead your target by a few feet to make the leap.

OBJECTIVES

* Avoid non-hostile casualties.

* Investigate tuna factory.

* Rescue factory workers.

* Find Gruber's missile.

You start on a ledge overlooking a warehouse area. Use your assault rifle to take out the mercenary threatening the factory worker with his flamethrower.

Use auto-jump to make the first leap onto the large blue crate below you. Then back up to fall to the ground. Grab the flamethrower and turn the switch on the control panel to start the crates moving.

Switch it on.

Item!

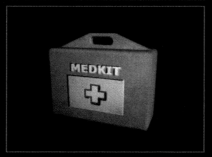

Before you use the brown crates to jump to the top level, go behind them to find a medkit. When you're done, climb up the crates.

Switch to the assault rifle, open the metal door and kill the two mercenaries on the other side of the pool. Step into the pool room, spin to your left and take out the guy on the near side.

Don't enter the pool room until the guys on the far side are dead.

Using the left trigger to steady your aim, shoot off the padlocks holding shut the cages on both sides. The metal drums will roll into the boiling oil.

Don't let him torch the hostage.

Using auto-jump, make the leap from barrel to barrel. It looks daunting, but if you line up your direction and make the jump, you'll easily cross.

Jump across in this order.

Item!

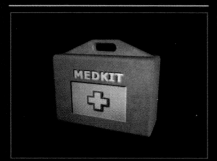

Open the door on the end and head down the stairs. When you see a medkit sitting on a barrel, be careful. There's a mercenary under the stairs across from the barrel, and he'll open fire on you. After you kill him, grab the medkit.

Watch out, there's a bad guy under the stairs behind you.

Open the next set of doors, crouch, and move behind the barrels on your right. The next doors pop open and three mercenaries will try to kill you. Eliminate them.

They'll get you if you're not ready.

Walk to the doors to the right to face another ambush. There's a mercenary behind a barrel to your right and another on the stairs above.

The guy on the stairs above can badly hurt you.

> ### TIP!
> Shoot the lower guy, back up, then make a run at the upper guy. This way, you'll avoid any crossfire.

Go up the stairs and open the door. You'll see a large conveyor belt. Jump down to it and let the fun begin.

Make sure your health is full.

The conveyor belt starts moving and pulling you toward grinders. Mercenaries shoot at you from above. Use Hero Mode. You should have a bunch of medkits saved up from the first part of this level.

In Hero Mode, it's easy.

> ### TIP!
> If you don't want to use Hero Mode, run forward, ignore most of the mercenaries, and jump the grinders. You'll take damage, but you'll live.

> ### TIP!
> Stay close to one side so you only have to worry about mercenaries on the opposite edge.

At the end of the conveyor is a ramp leading to another ledge. Use it and grab the tank of flamethrower fuel on the table above if you need it.

It's your ticket off the conveyor belt.

Item!

Jump over the conveyor pit and grab the medkit on the other side. Use auto-jump to avoid falling into the gap.

Check your health; you might need this.

Go through the door to find a short staircase. Back down the stairs and take out the two mercenaries hiding below you.

Another ambush.

Go through the next door, down the stairs, and through a door that opens into a big room containing a conveyor belt machine. There are a lot of mercenaries here, so be stealthy.

Take it slow, and crouch.

Crouch and sneak along the right side of the conveyor. When you reach the end, switch to the flamethrower, stand, and sneak toward the group while the leader is talking. When you're spotted, light up the group with the flamethrower.

> ## TIP!
> If you didn't use your Hero Points on the big conveyor belt, you can use them here to clean out the group.

Alternate Approach

If you wait on the right side of the conveyor belt machine, you can grab the mercenary leader (the guy in the hat) when he walks by after his speech. The only problem is that he won't tell his guys to surrender, he'll tell them to open fire.

Item!

When you're done, you'll find a pair of asbestos gloves on the table on the other side of the conveyor belt. Grab these for later.

Item!

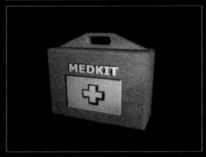

There's a medkit on the table next to the gloves.

PRIMA'S OFFICIAL STRATEGY GUIDE

Item!

If you ride the conveyor belt to the top level, you'll see a grenade pack on top of a stack of crates. Grab it.

Turn the wheel to open the steel door next to the spot where the mercenaries congregated. Turn the wheel on the next door to enter a room with an empty pool. You can't cross it empty.

Shoot holes in the water tank next to it and water pours out. Shoot the glass to fill the tank. When it's full, the crate floats to the top; jump to it, then jump to the other side.

Shoot lower along the glass to release more water.

Switch to your dual submachine guns and turn the crank to open the next door. You'll see another tank. There's a mercenary on top of it and a hostage drowning inside it. Shoot the bad guy.

Don't waste time; the hostage could drown.

When the mercenary is dead, shoot the bottom corner of the water tank with your dual submachine guns. Water runs out. Shoot until the hostage is above the water line. Don't shoot the hostage.

Item!

Run up the stairs above the tank to find an armor vest. You'll need its protection for the next leg of your journey.

Turn the crank to open the next door, and do the same thing to the door after it. Take a left to find a mercenary guarding the passage with a flamethrower. Take him out with the assault rifle.

Continue forward and open the next door. You're now in the freezer area. Shoot the Yakuza soldier.

Alternate Approach

You can take out the Yakuza guy easier by switching to Stealth Mode, shooting the liquid nitrogen tank next to him, and freezing him. Finish him off with a shot.

You'll come to another door with a frozen crank. Put on your asbestos gloves, use your flamethrower to heat the handle until it's no longer blue, and turn the crank to open the door.

Use the gloves so you don't burn your hands.

TIP!

Stand clear of the wall and door. If the flames bounce on you, you'll be damaged.

When the door opens, you face three Yakuza inside. Use the assault rifle and do not hit any liquid nitrogen tanks close to you. The cold spray will damage you.

The exit is locked from the outside. Stand clear and shoot the nearby liquid nitrogen tank, causing the door to freeze (it turns blue). When you shoot the frozen door, it shatters into pieces and you can proceed to the next section.

Level 8:
Cesar Tuna Factory

Cesar Tuna Factory: Part Three

OBJECTIVES

* Avoid non-hostile casualties.
* Investigate the tuna factory.
* Rescue the factory workers.
* Find Gruber's missile.

You start inside a corridor. Turn the crank on the door down the hall to your left to step into a large shipping yard.

Go to the top of the ramp. Turn 180 degrees to your left and squeeze between the big container and the back wall in Stealth Mode. Shoot the Yakuza on the other side of the container.

He won't see you coming.

Two other Yakuza troops spot you. Gun them down, then run toward where they came from, but don't go around the corner. Stay close to the red containers on your right.

Don't turn the corner.

As you approach the end of the container, another bad guy jumps out at you. Eliminate him, then edge out to your left. You see another Yakuza using a minigun. Take him out before he gets his gun up to speed.

Hit him, and he won't pull the minigun.

Spin around the corner of the red containers, but stick close to the wall. Eliminate the Yakuza standing in the yard. Aim your crosshairs at the same elevation as the Yakuza; your auto-targeting will lock on easier this way.

Aim here before you step out.

Slide to your left and use gunfire to take out the Yakuza on top of the crates in the distance with a rocket launcher. When you hit him, he'll launch a shot that hits the crane and sinks a yacht.

Fire the moment your crosshairs turn red and get out of the way.

When the boat sinks, reload and move forward. Two more Yakuza come at you. Shoot them. Move forward until you're near the first passage to the right, then back up. One Yakuza comes from the left side of the containers and another comes from the right passage.

Eliminate both Yakuza.

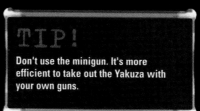

TIP!

Don't use the minigun. It's more efficient to take out the Yakuza with your own guns.

Follow the passage to the right and turn left at the first opening. You'll see another bad guy. Shoot him. Turn to your right and go the way you were headed until you reach the opening at the back wall. Turn left and take out the final Yakuza.

Item!

Return the way you came and take the first left (while facing the sunken yacht). You see a medkit and an armor vest. Grab them, turn around, and head toward the mercenaries and their two hostages.

Health and armor.

You'll run across the mercenaries and their hostages. Take out both mercenaries.

Alternate Approach

An easier way to take out the mercenaries is to shoot the silver bottom of the chute (there's caution tape around the lower edge) above and left of the hostages. It releases a truckload of dead fish that distracts the mercenaries enough to release their hostages.

Wait until the hostages are clear (give them a few seconds), then eliminate the mercenaries.

Talk to the two factory workers until they run. They'll lead you into the next area and activate the crane that lifts you into the warehouse. Follow them through several doors, then jump onto the boxes to get on the big green cargo trailer attached to the crane.

Get on top of the green trailer.

On your way up, shoot out the window and jump through it into the warehouse. Watch out for the guards patrolling below. Take a right and jump onto the lower red container.

Go this way, and you won't get hurt by the fall.

Navigate your way through the warehouse and take out the guards, either by arresting them or shooting them.

There are five guards; get them.

After all five guards are down, go to the big metal door. Switch to Stealth Mode and be sneaky. From this point on you must not be spotted. Push the button on the control panel to open the door.

Stay in Stealth Mode and sneak behind the containers on your left. Go around the left edge and sneak across the gap to the next set of containers (red). When a mercenary passes in front of you, grab him, and arrest him behind the containers.

First one down.

Return to the gap he came from and walk toward the semi. When you reach it, take a left to find another guard watching the door at the front of the truck. Grab him and drag him to a hidden spot on your left (facing outside).

Second one down.

Walk past the front of the truck to the other side of the warehouse. There is a ledge along the wall. Jump up to it and run (in Stealth Mode) around the corner to your right.

Here's the ledge.

Move down along the ledge in Stealth Mode until you're facing a blue container that's sitting next to a red container. Staying in Stealth Mode, jump onto the blue container.

Clear the gap.

After you're on top of the blue container, stay in Stealth Mode and jump up the wooden crates. Leap to the tall red and blue containers, but stay out of sight.

On top of the world.

VENDETTA™

Make a diagonal jump to the semi trailer and double-tap ⇓ to lie flat. Crawl to the open skylight, and wiggle to the front of the trailer to end the level.

Alternate Approach

Wait for the initial conversation between the two mercenaries to end. One mercenary walks around the corner, and the other stands guard at the back of the truck. Stay in stealth mode and shoot him in the head with your silenced pistol–any more than one shot to the head, and the others will come running; you will fail the mission. Run in stealth mode, and jump in the back of the truck.

Level 9:
Fernandez Warehouse

Fernandez Warehouse: Part One

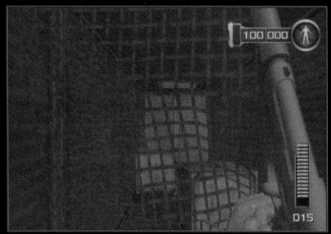

OBJECTIVES

* Find a way to avert the launch of Gruber's Missile.
* Rescue Lucy McClane.

You start in the back of a semi truck. When it stops moving, you hear a mercenary outside who opens the back door. Take him out and grab his assault rifle. Another bad guy is behind him, hidden from view by the large fuel tank.

There are four more mercenaries–one in the guard shack on your right (while facing the front gate), one behind the shack, one on a minigun in front of the semi, and one behind the minigunner. Take out the shooters, but don't get caught in the open in front of the minigun.

After you kill all the mercenary foot soldiers, head back to the semi trailer. Go to the nearest wall (facing the guard shack's front door). Keep that edge of the map directly to your right, and head toward the back of the map. Go slowly so you don't miss any hard-to-see openings.

Take out the first two.

The last guy may sneak up on you.

Follow this wall.

When you reach a point facing the back of another semi truck, take a sharp left to find the minigunner. It takes him a few moments to turn his gun in your direction. Kill him before he turns toward you.

Caught you sleeping.

Alternate Approach

You can start in Stealth Mode. Crouch and hide behind the last box in the trailer. When the mercenary says "Can someone check...", stand up and follow the other mercenary in Stealth Mode. Grab and arrest him.

Take the one on the left first.

When you're done, stay in Stealth Mode and follow the first mercenary behind the guard shack. Arrest him, then follow and arrest the next guard.

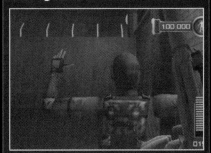

Three down without a sound.

You have to shoot through the other three and sneak back across the front gate and around the back side of the minigunner before shooting the other two.

Finish them off.

When all of the guards are dead, take some time to explore. You'll learn that the yard's exits are locked. You need to jump a fence.

How do you get over this fence?

Item!

Go to the guard shack. When you enter, locate the clipboard sitting on the counter. Grab it to learn how to keep Gruber from launching his rocket.

Bad guys keep notes.

You'll hear a trucker asking for someone to open the front gate. Activate the control panel on the counter to let the truck in. He parks in a convenient spot.

Don't worry about fighting the driver, he stays in his truck.

Item!

At the back of the guard shack is a medkit. Hopefully, you don't already need it.

Start saving these.

The semi parks in a spot that enables you to use it to leap over the fence. As you go toward the truck, locate the rocket fuel barrel sitting in the yard in front of a door.

The barrel in question.

From a distance, shoot the barrel to blow it up, then head to the stairs leading to the door behind it.

Kaboom!

Use the short stairs leading to the door and the porch to make the leap to the nearby container. Leap from the container to the semi, then over the fence.

Use auto-jump.

Take a right to see a door into the building. Stand in front of the window and wait until a mercenary passes by. Shoot him from the outside.

Sneaky.

Head down the building corridor until you hit another door. Look through the window to see two mercenaries. One is on the ground, the other is standing on some containers. Shoot them both without opening the door.

More window shots.

Go through the door to encounter a mercenary on the same containers, and another on the ground. Eliminate them both.

The last one dies in slow motion.

Turn left and move forward to find another rocket fuel barrel on the back wall. Take it out.

Stay at a safe distance when shooting the barrel.

Continue past the exploded fuel barrel to see a crate hanging from a cable and hear Lucy yelling. Before entering the area with the suspended cable, stop, turn around, and back in.

Turn around here–there's a bad guy behind and above you.

Back into the yard with your crosshairs targeted on the overhead catwalk. When you see the bad guy, take him out.

Don't let this guy ambush you.

Go to the control panel below the bad guy's perch, and turn on the crane. The box moves back and forth.

Crane switch.

When it's across from the crates on the other side of the yard, turn the switch again to stop the machine from moving. Use the crate to jump to the roof.

Stop it here.

Jump up the two crates on the yard's other side, and leap from the container onto the crate you just moved, then over to the roof.

Two short hops.

A mercenary is on the second, higher roof. Take him out from below. Don't go up the ladder; you can't shoot while you're climbing.

The roof guard is gone.

TIP!

Be careful, the guards can see you through the skylight glass.

Shoot out the glass on the two skylights on the lower roof. Three guards are in the room. Kill them all from above, or drop into the room and eliminate them.

Listen to them first for a hint about what's coming up next.

Item!

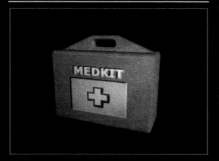

After all the guards are dead, find the medkit on one of the tables. Grab it and go.

More health.

Across from the table with the medkit is an unlocked door. Go through it, then up the stairs. Open the next door, then quickly back out. A dummy dressed like Lucy explodes.

Lucy?

Item!

It's not really Lucy and your game's not over. After the explosion, go into the room and grab the clipboard containing the keypad code.

The code you needed.

Return to the room you dropped into and use the action button on the keypad sitting next to the previously locked door. Go through the door and down the stairs to end this section of the level.

Use the action button to go through the door.

95

Level 9:
Fernandez Warehouse

Fernandez Warehouse: Part Two

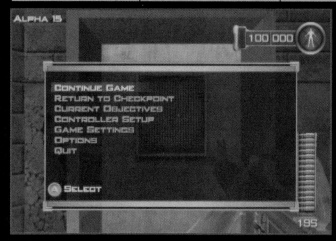

OBJECTIVES

* Destroy at least six fuel barrels.
* Rescue Lucy McClane.

You start at a door leading to a library. Stay left and work your way around the side of the room. When you reach the bookshelf against the left wall, turn right to see two mercenaries guarding the top of the stairs.

Take them out right away.

Stay where you are and kill two more guards as they climb the stairs into your line of fire. Don't approach the stairs until all four mercenaries are dead.

Stay back and they're easy to kill.

Item!

Go down the stairs and behind the staircase you'll find a medkit sitting on a desk.

Nice calendar.

Work your way around the room until you see a door. You'll hear music coming from that room. Enter and kill the two mercenaries inside after watching them dance for a while.

Bust a move.

Go through the other door at the top of the staircase. Head through the next room and out the other door. You should hear a toilet flushing. If you move quickly, you can shoot the mercenary as he exits the bathroom on the right.

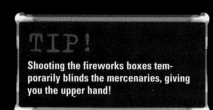

TIP!

Shooting the fireworks boxes temporarily blinds the mercenaries, giving you the upper hand!

Item!

When he's dead, turn around to see a medkit on the desk behind you. You should store this one without using it.

Another medkit...that means trouble.

Exit through the door opposite the bathroom to end up on a catwalk above a large room. Below are two mercenaries guarding another rocket fuel barrel. Kill them both.

Stay near the wall and take them out one at a time to avoid damage.

Alternate Approach

If you can make the shot, target the rocket fuel barrel and blow it up. Both mercenaries will die quickly.

Hopefully, mercenary insurance covers this kind of stuff.

Jump down to the lower floor and look for a door with a control panel beside it. Activate it to open the door. You'll hear two mercenaries on the balcony in the next room. Quietly slide into the room facing left and take them both out.

The guys should learn how to whisper.

Now shoot the panel that they were working on. The door on your right will open halfway. That's all you need to get through.

Don't go through yet.

Item!

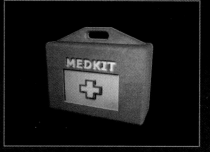

Under the fire hose reel is another medkit. Make sure you've got good health; a big battle is on the way.

A hose and a health.

The next room is loaded with bad guys, but the three on the catwalks above are your biggest threats. Crouch and maneuver to a spot from which you can hit the catwalk guard on the far left without entering the big room.

Tag him first.

Back away again while staying in the small room. Target the trooper on the ground to the right of the forklift. When he's dead, target the catwalk guard on your upper right side.

The second catwalk guard.

Next, edge over to the left side of the door until you pick up the last catwalk guard, who's located just to the left of the forklift.

Don't forget the third guard.

Stand up and run to the right side of the forklift and crates. Spin left to see another mercenary. Shoot him and the rocket fuel barrel beside him.

Only one more mercenary left.

While you're shooting at the previous guard, another one comes at you from ahead and to your right. Shoot him, too.

Last one down.

There's another rocket fuel barrel that you saw while running to your current position. Back out of the way and shoot it, too.

Five of ten.

Work toward the back of the room. As you do, you'll pass another rocket fuel barrel. Don't shoot it if you're standing next to a cardboard box of fireworks. They'll hurt you. Once you're past the cardboard box and in the clear, shoot the rocket fuel barrel.

Six of ten.

In the back of the room are some crates that step up to taller crates. Jump onto the taller crates, and at the end, jump diagonally to your left.

This will take you where you want to go.

Turn around, take two more diagonal jumps and then jump to the crates directly to the left (if facing the door you entered) of the forklift.

Stay left.

TIP!

Don't leave this room without destroying three rocket fuel barrels.

Jump up the crates onto the catwalk, then maneuver over the plank, back onto the catwalks, and out the door above where you entered. You have to make two jumps, but they're both easy.

Stay clear of the wall when jumping.

Go through several sets of doors until you reach an even larger storage room. You'll see a large loader below.

The big room.

Item!

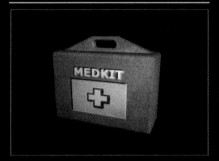

Look directly below the catwalk; you'll find a medkit sitting on a crate. Carefully jump down on top of it.

If you forget this, you can't go back for it.

Drop to the floor, and head left along the wall. Turn right at the loader and you'll hear a mercenary struggling with another fuel barrel. Shoot the barrel or the mercenary.

Seven of ten.

Use the action button on the control panel to start the loader moving. Immediately run to the loader and hop onto the lift. If you don't go quickly, you'll miss it and have to wait until it returns.

Switch and run.

Ride the lift and kill the two mercenaries that you encounter. Be careful shooting the fuel barrel while you're next to it on the lift. It will damage you badly if you're not on the back side of the lift.

The explosion may take out the second mercenary.

The lift takes you all the way over to the catwalk on the far wall. Leap out when the lift starts moving in the other direction.

On to the control room.

Go up the stairs and around the corner into the control room. When you see a poster below a large fan, shoot into the opening on the left. A guard will pop out to investigate the noise. Shoot him.

Who's surprised now?

Use the action button to activate the control panel on the far side of the control room. This turns on the loader on the other side.

Now they're both working.

Item!

Another medkit is sitting just below the control panel. Don't forget it.

More meds.

Return to the catwalk and leap onto the lift when it comes close. Ride the lift back to the spot where you destroyed the fuel barrel. There should be a large hole in the wall because of the explosion.

Property damage.

Crouch and crawl through the hole. A guard on your left will spot you. Kill him and then jump on the next loader when it approaches.

Another ride.

Ride the lift down and take out the mercenary hiding among the crates in the lower middle section. When the lift reaches its farthest point, leap onto the top of the window looking into the control panel.

Make sure you have full health before you try this leap.

Turn around, back up to the wall, run, and make the leap to the roof of the storage structure. Climb the ladder up to the air vents.

Up you go.

Immediately switch to Stealth Mode, double-tap ⇓ to lie prone and slowly make your way across the vents toward the exit. Follow the path listed on this map to make it safely.

JUMP
JUMP JUMP
JUMP

Switch to Action Mode and stand only when making a leap.

> ## TIP!
>
> While trying to jump in Action Mode, have your weapon activated so you can use the crosshairs to precisely control your direction.

Jump from the last section of the vent down to the catwalk with the grate at the end. Stay clear of the wall so that you don't hook on a column and fall to your death.

Last leap to safety.

Shoot out the vent and crawl through it to exit this section of the level.

Another day, another vent.

Level 9:
Fernandez Warehouse

Fernandez Warehouse: Part Three

* **Destroy at least 10 fuel barrels.**
* **Initiate conveyor belt system.**

You drop into a room where you'll immediately face a mercenary trying to run you down with a forklift. Stand up, turn around, and run behind one of the crates.

You'll need these soon enough.

Switch into Stealth Mode and jump on top of a crate. Wait until the forklift comes toward you, then jump on top of, or over, the container that it's pushing.

Item!

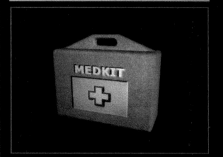

Activate the control panel on the far wall and open the door. Go into the next room to find a medkit in the corner next to a chair.

Nine of ten.

Carefully inch back and take out the two catwalk guards on the room's upper right side. Move back to safety behind the right door frame.

Up and over.

Store these.

Activate the control panel on the next door to open the next room. Two guards are on the ground close to a fuel barrel; two more are in the catwalks. Shoot the fuel barrel to take out the ground troops, then slide behind the door frame.

Shoot and dodge.

Slide to the door's left side to see another guard on the rear catwalk, left of the center pillar. Take him out.

101

Another guard down.

Turn around and back into the room to take out the final guard who's hiding in the catwalk above the door. When you kill the last guard, a death sequence plays.

This room's clear.

Item!

Walk to the room's middle, load up on ammo, and grab the medkit that's sitting on a crate.

No lack of medkits here.

The conveyor belt isn't working, but the switch is on the catwalk. Return to the entrance and climb the ladder to get to the upper level.

Up again.

Item!

Before you go around the catwalk, exit through the upper door on the wall, then take a quick right to see a bad guy. Shoot him and take his night vision goggles.

Grab these!

Return to the catwalks. It's too far to jump, but you'll notice some big inflatable balloons. Shoot one of them once so it slowly loses air and falls. Use the falling balloon as a platform to jump across. It's difficult, but you can do it.

The penguin is the easiest.

TIP!

Don't jump too early. Jump when the balloon is below you, then jump again to get across.

When you get across, activate the control panel to get the conveyor belt started, then jump on it. Ride along the belt, shooting all the mercenaries and fuel barrels you encounter. Keep up your health.

Ten of ten barrels.

Here's a quick reference table of what you'll encounter:

Room 1: Nothing
Room 2: Mercenary (ahead); fuel barrel (ahead and left); two mercenaries (ahead and right)
Room 3: Nothing
Room 4: Mercenary (ahead); mercenary (left)
Room 5: Mercenary (right)
Room 6: Mercenary (behind and to the right); mercenary (behind and to the left)

TIP!

Constantly check your health while you're on the conveyor; use a medkit whenever your health points drop to near or below 50.

Item!

When the conveyor belt brings you to floor level, hop off to find a medkit next to where the ramp hits the floor level of the conveyor.

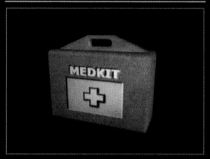

Make sure you're at 100 health.

Use the control panel to open the door out of the room, take a quick right, and take out the mercenaries who are moving the fuel barrels. Shoot the fuel barrels for some pyrotechnics.

Big boom.

Head into the next room to hear two mercenaries arguing. Use the control panel to open the next door, then kill them both. A third and fourth mercenary are to the right of them. Kill them, too.

Amateur arbitration.

After a short cinematic, you'll face Marlin. She is deadly, and you don't have any Hero Points stored, so take her out carefully.

Marlin's fast.

Get in a spot where your back is covered and you can tag her when she runs along the top ledge. One such spot is to the left of the forklift (facing its front). Get your back in a corner between the wall and one of the pillars.

Camp here.

Keep your eye on the front wall and watch your health and ammo. If you were careful, you have plenty of both to spare. Kill Marlin and the level's done.

Aim for the head.

Level 10:
Nakatomi Plaza

Nakatomi Plaza: Part One

OBJECTIVES

* **Rescue Lucy.**
* **Get Gruber.**
* **Avoid non-hostile casualties.**

You begin at the base of Nakatomi Plaza. Immediately run up and talk with Al. He tells you that Lucy is inside and asks you to lead the SWAT team.

Here again.

Go through the revolving doors, run past the SWAT team, toward the gates that drop on the other side. Mercenaries will grenade the SWAT team.

You're safer over here.

Two mercenaries are on each side of the crossing hallway. Take all four out with your combat shotgun and grab their weapons. The first two walk into your line of fire. When they're dead, take out the two on your right.

Don't get caught in the crossfire.

Go to the hallway with six elevators and walk to the farthest one on the right. Activate the control panel and jump inside.

Last elevator going up.

Step out of the elevator and walk toward the laptop. A short cinematic plays and part one of this level ends.

This doesn't look promising.

Nakatomi Plaza: Part Two

When the cinematic ends, you have 15 seconds to find a way out of the office. Run to the far end of the office to a window that's slightly ajar. Use the action button to open it.

Get me out of here.

Jump through the open window into the window washer cart. Crouch and activate the button at the far end of the cart. You'll start downward.

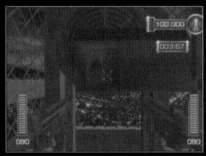

Hurry, hurry.

Above you, the entire floor explodes, but you're safe. Jump through the opened window on the floor below.

Back inside.

Go through the offices until you reach the main hallway. Take a right and pass an exit door on your left. It's locked. Go to the hallway's end to see four doors (two on the right, one at the end, and one on the left).

Choose the door on the left.

Item!

Go through the left door. A mercenary is inside. Kill him and grab the medkit in the room behind him.

Coffee and Band-Aids.

Return to the office where you started and, take a left into the hallway. Run across an elevator bank and shoot the mercenary guarding this area.

Time to move on.

Go to the elevator on the left side and open it using the control panel. A mercenary is inside; shoot him and take the elevator up.

Sorry, this is my ride.

When you reach the 23rd floor, turn right to see two mercenaries in an office at the end of a hallway. Kill them.

Dead meat.

Item!

When you enter the office at the hallway's end, turn left as you go through the door. Kill the bad guy and take his walkie-talkie.

Ten-four, good buddy.

All the other doors in this hallway are locked, so head to the elevator and up to the next floor.

It's getting hotter.

105

Alternate Approach

If you don't want to make your way up floor-by-floor, hit the down button and jump out before the elevator goes down.

John McClane and the Nakatomi elevator shaft, together again.

When it drops to the next floor, jump onto the top of the elevator, use the control panel that sends the elevator up, and head to the top avoiding the battles below.

Upward controls are on the right.

When you reach the 25th floor, shoot out the emergency shaft panel and drop into the elevator. Watch for mercenaries; they're heavily guarding the elevator.

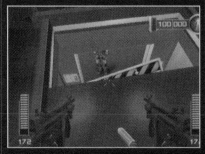

Very sneaky.

On the next floor, go left when the elevator opens. Two mercenaries are to your left, and one is on a minigun. Shoot them quickly.

Don't let the minigun get started.

Item!

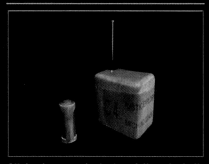

All the doors are locked, so follow the hallway around the first two left corners. You encounter a mercenary setting a C4 charge. Kill him and grab the C4 and a trigger.

Tasty explosives.

Get on the elevator and head to the 25th floor. Shoot the minigun shooter on your left. Grab his gun and aim it on the second elevator to the right.

Start shooting early.

If you've got the gun revved up, aim into the elevator entrance to kill all the guards as they walk through the door.

Mow them down.

Grab their weapons and spin around the next corner to the left. There's another minigun; kill the mercenary who's manning it.

Shoot quickly and get out of the way.

All the doors are locked except the exit at the hallway's end. Take this exit to go to the level's next section.

The end of part two.

Nakatomi Plaza: Part Three

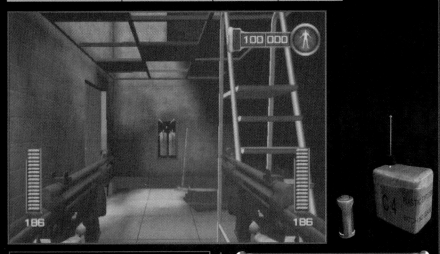

Through the next latticed door are two mercenaries, one directly to your right and another to your far right around a wall. Shoot them, then go through the next set of doors.

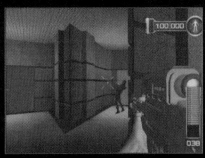

This last guy's easy to miss.

OBJECTIVES

* **Rescue Lucy.**
* **Get Gruber.**
* **Avoid non-hostile casualties.**

You start in a stairwell to the maintenance room. Go through the open door and up the stairs until you reach the top. Go through the next door to an office corridor lined with locked doors and take a right. Follow the far wall until you see a latticed door.

TIP!

Latticed doors are unlocked (except for one door we'll mention later).

When you go through the door, take a right to see a mercenary. Take him out and grab his high-powered assault rifle.

In the next room, there's a partition on your right. An enemy is hiding behind it. Shoot him, and continue through the next set of doors.

The only unlocked door.

He won't see you.

Bang.

You'll see the only non-latticed door that isn't locked at the end of the next room. Open it and step to one side of the doorway to avoid fire from the minigun at the room's end. Three mercenaries are near you. One is on the left, and the other two are on the right.

Take out all three without entering the room.

Go into the room; go to the right to avoid the minigun's fire. Keep the columns between you and the open door until you reach the column closest to the shooters.

Here's the safe spot.

Edge out and kill the mercenary in the left rear corner of the room. Take out the minigunner and the two guys behind him. Be patient and use your scope.

Peek and fire.

TIP!

You can kill some of the guys in the next room by targeting and shooting them through the water cooler while crouching behind it.

Alternate Approach

Shoot the wire dangling from the ceiling, then shoot the fire alarm. The sprinklers and wire combo electrocutes everyone inside.

Shocking.

The entire room is electrified, so jump onto the desks. Walk along the tops and jump to the desk on the room's far side. Jump to the back corner near the door. You're safe.

Not so safe a leap.

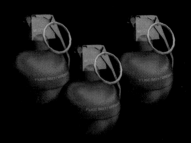

TIP!

Unless you're a glutton for punishment, skip this approach. It's difficult because the jumping is iffy; you die if you miss a leap.

Item!

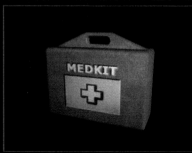

Go through the double glass doors into a large office with sofas and tables. Grab the medkit on the table to your left. Be careful, sometimes a bad guy is on your right.

Go through the next set of glass doors and past the elevators. There are latticed doors to your right. Go through them, then go through the exit door.

More stairs.

As soon as you reach the stairs, look up and kill the mercenary waiting for you halfway up the first flight of steps. Climb to the top and head through the door. When you go through the next door, two bad guys are waiting for you, one in front of you and another to your right.

If you didn't get the walkie-talkie earlier, get it now.

All the doors are locked except for the double lattice doors. They open to an office containing five mercenaries. From outside the room, kill them all.

Dodge behind the door frame while reloading.

Go through the next set of glass doors, then through a dark brown single door. The first latticed doorway on your left contains a mercenary. Eliminate him.

He tells Gruber that you're coming.

Item!

Go into the room where the mercenary died to find a medkit.

Thanks for leaving this, buddy.

Go through either set of the double latticed doors, and kill the two mercenaries inside. Go through either set of the glass doors, take a left, and go through the single latticed door.

Go through carefully.

When you enter the next room, a screen is set up in front of you. Move forward and it drops, revealing a minigunner and another mercenary. Kill them.

Shoot when the screen drops.

Item!

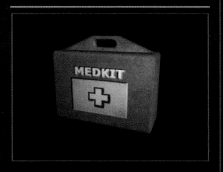

Go through the latticed door on the room's other side to enter a hallway with double glass doors. Take the one on the left to get a medkit.

Go through the other double glass door and kill the mercenary in the elevator bank. Go into the hallway and kill another mercenary who is to your right.

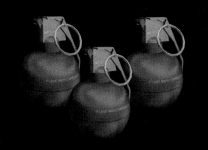

Guarding the exit.

Go through the latticed exit door and enter the elevator. Hit the up control panel to exit this section of the level.

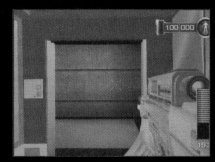

The final ride up.

Level 10:
Nakatomi Plaza

Nakatomi Plaza: Part Four

OBJECTIVES

* **Rescue Lucy.**
* **Get Gruber.**
* **Avoid non-hostile casualties.**

You start in an elevator, where you're immediately attacked. Prepare for the ambush and start firing first.

Let's do this.

Spin left to confront four more mercenaries. Kill them quickly.

If you need to, jump back into the elevator to reload.

Take a right at your first opportunity, but don't take the second right. You'll see a latticed door on the left wall. Enter it and talk with Lucy.

She's alive!

Item!

A medkit is sitting on a desk behind Lucy. Grab it and use it if you need to.

A daughter and a medkit.

As soon as you approach Lucy, the timer on the bomb strapped around her waist starts ticking. You have two minutes to find the detonator code. Don't get in a rush, you have plenty of time.

Time's a-wasting.

Leave through the door closest to Lucy. Turn left and kill the mercenary in front of you. Go straight and take two right turns until you're facing the room's large open area. Shoot the mercenary on the ground near the fountain.

Two down.

Slide to the right with your back against the wall and take out the two mercenaries halfway up the stairs. Spin around, back out, and kill the mercenary in the balcony that was directly above you.

Three, four, and five.

Item!

Climb the stairs and take out the two mercenaries hiding in the office. One of them will drop the detonator code. Grab it and head back to Lucy.

Six and seven.

When you reach Lucy, open your inventory and activate the detonator code near her. She'll be free and the timer will stop.

TIP!

Keep a sharp eye on your health. You'll take a lot of hits in this section, but you should have some medkits saved.

Best dad ever!

Follow her to the second elevator and press Ⓐ. When you exit, you'll see a locked door. Try to open it and Lucy will punch in the code.

Teamwork.

Step out of the doorway and turn quickly to your right. Shoot the mercenary in your way and start sprinting around the top of the building in a clockwise motion. You'll have to kill at least three mercenaries in front of you.

Run and gun.

If you stop or even slow down, you run the risk of getting caught in a crossfire, and that spells certain death for Lucy. Keep running until a cutscene starts. Only one more level to go.

Level 11:
THE HOLMES OBSERVATORY

The Holmes Observatory: Part One

OBJECTIVES

* **Apprehend Frontier.**
* **Free any hostages you encounter.**
* **Avoid non-hostile casualties.**

You start at the main gates of the Holmes Observatory. Switch to Stealth Mode, turn right, and hang alongside the right wall. The bad guys won't see you there.

Stay out of trouble at the start.

Sneak to the crates to find a rocket launcher. Switch to the assault rifle and stay in Stealth Mode.

Grab the rocket launcher, switch guns, and keep moving.

Turn left (you'll face the large yard). There are three sets of two mercenaries crouching in the distance. Sneak toward them.

You'll have to fight your way through these guys.

Do not stop in one place. The remote-controlled rocket launchers on top of the base will spot you if you stop. If you keep moving, they won't hit you.

You've been spotted.

Continue toward the ground troops and line up the two closest sets in a straight line. When you reach the light post halfway between the crates and the first troops, open fire and take them out.

If you line up the mercenaries first, it's easier to get them.

Run toward the middle set of mercenaries while you're shooting at the other bad guys. There is more rocket launcher ammo in the spot where the middle guys were.

Don't miss the rocket launcher ammo.

When you grab the rocket launcher ammo, move toward the base of the observatory, shooting the remaining mercenaries. The farthest of the six mercenaries is the last one to die.

When you kill the last one, you'll see a death sequence.

Continue toward the building until you are next to it. Here you are safe from the remote-controlled rocket launchers and the helicopter above. Stay alongside the building until you are on the left side of the entrance.

You're safe here.

The helicopter is shooting at you, but is missing over your head by a long distance. Switch to the rocket launcher, back away from the building, and unleash a rocket at the helicopter. Move to safety.

Take your time and get a clean shot from the safety of the building's edge.

When you hit the helicopter, it smokes and crashes. This opens a door in the back left corner near you.

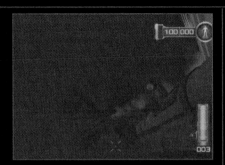

Item!

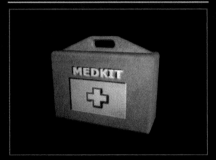

Jump inside the burning wreck to find a medkit on the back wall. You may need to use it.

Stay clear of the fire.

Go through the now-open door and make sure you're fully reloaded. Follow the hallway around the corners and up the long flight of stairs. Crouch when you reach the top.

Do not get spotted.

Staying crouched, crawl along the roof until you reach another set of stairs. Switch into Stealth Mode and edge around the building to your right until you see two guards standing next to a big spotlight.

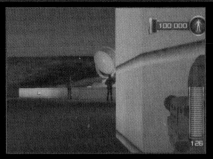

Take out these guys.

Shoot them from a distance or shoot out the spotlight and they'll both go flying. Slide behind the building.

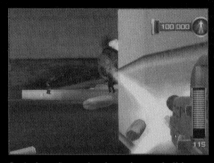

Switch to the rocket launcher and slide out farther. You'll see a remote-controlled rocket launcher. Hit it with your rocket before it shoots at you.

Make it quick or you'll eat a rocket.

Item!

Crawl to the two dead mercenaries, pick up their ammo, and grab the circuit breaker that one of them drops. You'll need it to disarm bombs later.

Remember this from the training level?

Crawl along to the left of the next rooftop and edge out when you reach the side peeking to the front of the building.

Go around the left, but stay close to the building's side.

When you reach the next corner, edge out to spot two more mercenaries. Don't shoot the spotlight yet. First, hit the remote-controlled rocket launcher with a rocket to deactivate it.

Go for the launcher first.

The explosion takes out one of the two mercenaries. Shoot out the spotlight to eliminate the remaining one. Keep crouching.

The last rooftop mercenary.

115

Crawl to the spotlight and take a left. You'll see a door next to the telescope tower. It's locked. You'll need to get a key.

We'll come back here later.

With your back against the rocket launcher, stand up. Run to the short wall ahead of you and jump onto the rooftop below.

Jump over this short wall to the right of the gap.

After you hit the lower rooftop, move forward and jump to the next lower rooftop, then to the ground.

Don't get caught on the ledge.

Move forward through the balcony on your left until you see a mercenary. Shoot him, stop, and crouch.

Don't get too close; there's a proximity mine beside him.

Turn around, stand, then double tap your crouch button to lie prone. Belly crawl toward the way you came and pick off the six mercenaries in the courtyard below you (including one with a minigun).

Take your time.

TIP!

Your auto-target will pick up bad guys through plants. You can shoot the mercenaries through the plants and they won't see you.

Item!

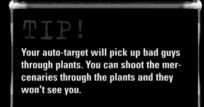

When all six mercenaries are dead (you may have to run at the two farthest ones), walk into the courtyard and talk to the wounded security guard sitting along one of the walls. Talk with him until he gives you a set of master keys.

This gets you into the locked door you found earlier.

Item!

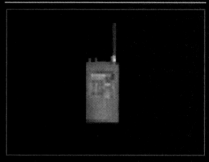

If you keep talking, the security guard hands you his walkie talkie, then dies. Activate the walkie talkie to contact Captain Al.

Return to the circular balcony and go around the building. There are two proximity mines planted on the left wall along the way—one by the first mercenary you killed when you jumped to this area, and another by the next mercenary on the balcony.

Shoot the proximity mine before you get close enough for it to go off.

Stop when you see an opening on the short railing to your right. Switch to Stealth Mode and sneak forward, looking to the right. More mercenaries are standing in the parking lot below you. Shoot the one on the minigun, then crouch.

Use the element of surprise to take out the minigunner first.

Move forward until you kill another mercenary who's on the balcony past the opening.

Two of six dead.

Back up until you can see the opening, then wait until the other four mercenaries climb the stairs. Pick them off one at a time before they shoot back.

Get all six in this area.

As you go down the stairs, look forward and up to see a rope and a pulley holding a cargo crate. Shoot the pulley and the crate falls.

Shoot the pulley, not the rope.

Climb up the rope that was holding the crate to get behind the remote control rocket launchers you previously destroyed. Take a left and go to the locked door below the telescope dome.

Back on the roof again.

Open your inventory, activate the circuit breaker, and go through the door that was locked.

Activate the circuit breaker.

When you walk in, you'll see a suitcase bomb. As you approach it, it beeps and you'll see a code. Use the corresponding buttons to type in the code before the timer runs out.

The code changes each time you encounter it.

Item!

After you disarm the bomb, walk into the next room and pick up the medkit on the table to your right.

You need this now.

A control panel is on the right side of the room. Use your action button on it to turn off the remote controlled rocket launchers you destroyed and give power to the telescope mover.

If you didn't destroy the rocket launchers, this shuts them off.

Turn to your left to find a control panel labeled dome control panel. Use your action button on it; your view automatically shifts to a nearby screen. Use your right joystick to turn the telescope until the ladder is on top of the nearby roof.

Spin it 90 degrees clockwise.

Go outside the room, turn right, and go to the side opposite the door you just used. Use the ledges to jump on top of the room you were just in, then climb the ladder to the top of the telescope dome.

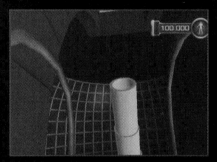

Top of the world.

Jump to the top of the telescope, and climb down the other side. You'll see a set of stairs going down. Take the stairs and stop when you reach the bottom level.

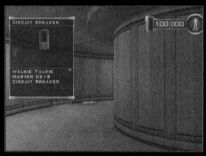

Oops, another bomb.

Switch to your circuit breaker and approach the bomb. Disarm it using the code when the timer starts. When you disarm the bomb, head through the door behind it, and proceed to the next section.

Be quick.

Level 12:
THE HOLMES OBSERVATORY

The Holmes Observatory: Part Two

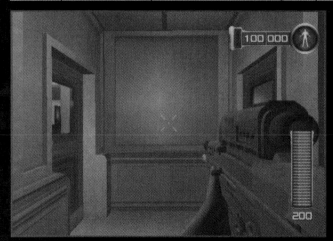

OBJECTIVES

* Defeat Frontier.

* Free any hostages you encounter.

* Avoid non-hostile casualties.

* Deactivate suitcase bombs.

* Open shutter doors to dining hall.

You start in a hallway with two doors at the end. Switch into Action Mode, and you should already have a target locked on through the window of the left door. Shoot that mercenary, circle to your right, and shoot two more through the window.

Don't even go into the room yet.

Open the door and kill the guard to the left of the entrance. Exit, reload, and kill the two guards at the far end of the room on your right.

Kill all six mercenaries in this room.

Item!

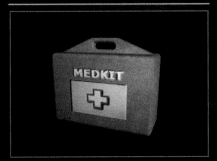

There's a medkit in the far right corner of the room. Grab it.

Tough levels require lots of medkits.

Go through the next door and follow the hall until it makes a right turn. There's a mercenary waiting for you around that corner. Take him out and go to the next door.

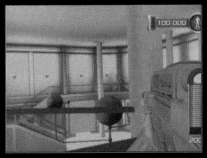

You can see a bad guy through the window.

Shoot the mercenary in the next room through the window. Slide to the right side of the window and shoot another mercenary on the left side of the door outside.

Another window shot.

Enter the room and kill the guard behind a pillar on your right side. Go downstairs and through the beige double doors.

Keep moving this way.

When you open the door, Jesse Montana runs up to talk to you. Run past her (and the smoke grenade the bad guys throw), and take out the two mercenaries hiding on both sides of the last displays in the hallway.

There's one on each side here. Be careful.

Turn back to the way you were headed to see four mercenaries coming through the door at the room's far end. Mow them down.

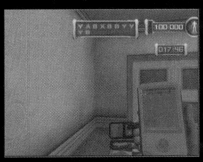

Don't get close to them or the bomb will start to go off.

Once the mercenaries are dead, open your inventory, select your circuit breaker, and approach the bomb near the far door. Disarm it carefully.

Don't panic, you have plenty of time.

Go through the door to a room with a large red column in it. On the back side of the column is a vent. Shoot it out, go through it, and jump to the ladder inside. Climb all the way down to the ground floor.

Grates and ladders.

Go through the door, take out the mercenary ahead and to your left, and then go to the end of the hall, turn right and take out the next one.

Ooh, a flamethrower.

Around the next corner to the right, you'll encounter two mercenaries behind a barricade. Take them down. Go to the end of that hallway, take another right, and kill the mercenary waiting for you at the end of that passage.

Note the door on your left.

There are five mercenaries in the room just past the short hall to your left. Take them out from a distance by shooting and dodging from side to side.

Take care of them now instead of later.

Go back to the hallway you were just in and you'll see a door to the right. Go a foot or two inside the door, and kill the mercenary hiding on the right.

If you go in too far, you'll start the bomb timer.

Alternate Approach

If you don't want to risk setting off the bomb, just shoot one of the boxes inside this room and the guard will come to you.

Draw him out.

Switch to the circuit breaker again, enter the room, and disarm the bomb. You have more time than you think.

Be precise.

Item!

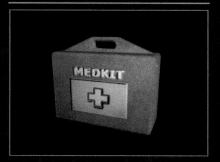

In the back corner of the room (directly across from the door) is a well-hidden medkit. Grab it now.

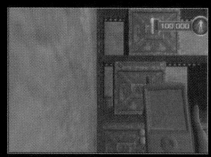

Hard to find.

Go back through the room where you killed the five mercenaries. Head through two doors and down a set of stairs. At the bottom of the stairs is a doorway. Go through it, spin right, and kill the mercenary waiting for you behind another barricade.

This guy was well set up.

Continue until you reach a generator room with fences between you and some mercenaries. Shoot through the fences to get all five. One is on the ground to your right and two others are up above you on top of the fences.

Don't forget the guys up above.

Weave through the room until you reach some pipes that you have to duck under. Crawl under them and then shoot the fourth mercenary on the ground to your left.

You've nailed the fourth one.

Item!

A medkit is between the wall and the fourth generator you pass.

First aid.

Continue until you have to make a 180-degree right turn. The fifth and final mercenary in this room is on top of the fence at the far end of the hall.

Last one down.

Go down the hall and through the door on your right. You'll see another door and a mercenary through the window. Shoot the mercenary, open the door, spin to the left, and kill the other mercenary in the room.

Two more hiding.

You'll see a control switch in the back corner of the room. Switch it to open the shutter doors to the dining hall.

Soup's on.
Leave the office, go back down the hall, and head through the large double doors on the far left. Go up the stairs and switch to Stealth Mode as soon as you reach the top.

Trouble on your left.

Sneak through the left doors to find three mercenaries holding some hostages. Line yourself up so that you can get a clean shot (no hostages in the line of fire) at the two mercenaries closest to the hostages. Kill them both and then kill the farthest one.

Make the first two kills quickly and carefully.

Immediately grab your circuit breaker and disarm the fifth and final bomb in the back of the room. Only then should you talk with the hostages.

It's easy to start the bomb timer while talking to the hostages.

The double doors are still locked. Go and shoot the globe from the back to make it roll through the doors. There are two mini-gunners at the far end. Take them out.

PRIMA'S OFFICIAL STRATEGY GUIDE

Get the ball rolling.

Alternate Approach

You can go to the big room opposite the way you came. It takes longer, but you won't have to deal with the minigunners.

You could take the long way around.

Run to the minigun and turn around. A wave of mercenaries comes running at you. Take them out with the minigun or the assault rifle.

The assault rifle will do the trick nicely.

Now you're back in the large room with the rotating planets. Go through the beige-and-pink double doors to end this part of the level.

You're almost done.

Level 12:
THE HOLMES OBSERVATORY

The Holmes Observatory: Part Two

You start on the upper level of a large room. Crouch so no one on the lower floor can see you. Crawl to your left, and switch to the assault rifle.

OBJECTIVES

* Defeat Frontier.
* Avoid non-hostile casualties.

The final level begins.

When you hear McClane say "Show's over, Frontier," watch the left stairs. A mercenary will soon appear. Kill him as quickly as possible.

Shoot and then turn right.

The second he's dead, turn right and shoot the mercenary who shows up atop the stairs on the other side. Continue to the top of that stairwell while reloading. Stop clear of the right stairwell and wait for mercenaries.

Get in position.

Watch carefully, because the first two people to come to the top of the stairs are a mercenary and a civilian. The mercenary will stop at the top of the stairs, the civilian will keep going…and sometimes stand in front of you.

Identify your target before shooting.

Eliminate the mercenary near the hostage and stay in position to wipe out the next three bad guys as they climb the stairs after the first bad guy.

Stay in position until they're all down.

Item!

Run down the stairs and head to the door in the rear left corner of the room. Grab the medkit that's sitting on a table.

You'll really want this in a minute.

Go through the next set of double doors and turn right. The opening to the left leads to a large auditorium and a very angry Frontier.

The final showdown.

Unload a couple of clips from your assault rifle into his head. When he dies, pick up his minigun.

The last Frontier.

Alternate Approach

If you don't want to use hero points, fight him in the hallway and make a run for the upper rim of the auditorium.

Run at him, spin left, duck, and head up one of the aisles.

When you reach the upper rim, you'll see medkits and explosive ammo. Run around the rim in either direction to set off the proximity mines without getting hurt. Don't grab anything on your first lap, just set off the mines. Get as much as you can on your second lap.

Stay a little outside the middle of the aisle and keep moving.

Now you should be ready to fight him. Watch your health and ammo, and attack while dodging his shots. If you have good aim and you make plenty of head shots, you can kill this difficult foe.

Hard work, but worth the effort.

As soon as he's dead, switch into Hero Mode, run up to the upper ring, and go through the right side exit. Run to the first door, and shoot it with the assault rifle or Frontier's minigun.

Run and gun.

> # TIP!
> **Turn on Auto Weapon Switch to save time.**

In the next room, run to the double doors you entered through and shoot them, too. Finally, shoot through the large front doors and run outside. Congratulations, you've made it!

Fin.

Secrets

If you've made it through *Die Hard: Vendetta* and haven't uncovered these great secrets, go back and check them out!

The Flower Pot Trick

Found In: The Townsend Museum

At the end of this level, a mercenary guards Lucy McClane at gunpoint. Rather than killing him with the sniper rifle, target one of the flowerpots above his head. When you shoot it, it falls and distracts him long enough for you to get a clean shot.

Raining Money

Found In: Hollywood Boulevard

As you run in front of the bank, you'll see a gang member holding a hostage. Forget taking him out; instead shoot the ATM view screen to his left. The ATM explodes and sends money flying everywhere. The hapless criminal is so distracted by the flying cash, that he forgets about his hostage.

Changing Room Mishap

Found In: Hollywood Boulevard

After you take out the gang members inside the Fashion Outlet, go to the four changing booths in the back of the store. One of them contains a gang member whom you need to kill. Another has a lady who's not fully dressed; she's not happy to see you.

Music Clerk Hints

Found In: Hollywood Boulevard

Go into the music store before going into the Fashion Outlet and find the music clerk. A gang member crouches behind the desk, guarding him. Watch him squirm and hint that someone's pointing a gun at him. Eventually the gang member pops up and you can kill him.

Movie Magic

Found In: Film Studio

At the end of the Film Studio level's first part is a box of blank minigun ammo. In the next section, you'll run across a couple of mercenaries holding some actors hostage. Activate the minigun to scare the mercenaries and free the actors.

Poster Girl

Found In: The Sierra Correctional Facility

Hanging on the wall in one of the prison psych ward cells is a poster of a woman in a bikini. If you hit Ⓐ on the poster, it falls to reveal a tunnel into an area behind the cells.

Master Keys

Found In: The Sierra Correctional Facility

The Warden keeps his master keys hidden behind a painting on the wall. You'll make this discovery if you're inquisitive while searching the room, and you'll appreciate these hidden keys.

Suicidal Leader

Found In: Cesar Tuna Factory

Usually when you capture a mercenary leader, he's willing to help you and tell his buddies to surrender. However, in the Cesar Tuna Factory, you find a mercenary leader who takes his job seriously enough to order his troops to open fire on you, even though it assures his death.

Hasta La Vista

Found In: Cesar Tuna Factory

While fighting through the tuna factory, you'll enter a freezer room with a bunch of liquid nitrogen tanks. A Yakuza soldier sits next to one of these tanks. Instead of shooting the soldier, shoot the tank next to him and he freezes. Hit him with a bullet, and he shatters.

The Shaft

Found In: Nakatomi Plaza

As you head up through the floors of the Nakatomi building, you'll leave an elevator and realize that the doors don't shut all the way. Instead of going up through this elevator the next time around, hit the down button and jump out before the interior doors close. Turn around to see the elevator drop, leaving the shaft open. Jump in to relive the first *Die Hard* movie.